Present with Suffering

Being with the Things that Hurt

For all sentient beings

Nigel Wellings and
Elizabeth Wilde McCormick

Present with Suffering

Being with the Things that Hurt

First published in 2022 by Confer books, an imprint of Confer Ltd

www.confer.uk.com

Registered office:
Brody House, Strype Street, London E1 7LQ

Copyright © 2022 Nigel Wellings
Copyright © 2022 Elizabeth Wilde McCormick

The right of Nigel Wellings and Elizabeth Wilde McCormick to be identified as the authors of this work has been asserted by them in accordance with sections 77 and 78 of the Copyright, Designs and Patents Act, 1988.

All rights reserved. No part of this document may be reproduced or transmitted in any form or by any means, electronic, mechanical, photocopying, recording, or otherwise, without prior written permission of the copyright owner.

This is a work of nonfiction. Any similarity between the characters and situations within its pages, and places, persons, or animals living or dead, is unintentional and co-incidental. Some names and identifying details may have been changed or omitted to protect the privacy of individuals. Every effort has been made to trace the copyright holders and obtain permission to reproduce this material. If you have any queries or any information relating to text, images or rights holders, please contact the publisher.

British Library Cataloguing in Publication Data
A catalogue record for this book is available from the British Library.

ISBN: 978-1-913494-44-5 (paperback)
ISBN: 978-1-913494-45-2 (ebook)

Typeset by Bespoke Publishing Ltd.
Printed in the UK by Ashford Colour Press.

CONTENTS

LIST OF MEDITATIONS	vii
FOREWORD *by Henry Schukman*	ix
ACKNOWLEDGEMENTS	xiii
INTRODUCTION *by Nigel Wellings*	xvii

PRESENT WITH SUFFERING IN LOSS AND BEREAVEMENT
by Elizabeth Wilde McCormick — 1

Impermanence and attachment	3
The human body in loss and bereavement	21
Heart	39
Mind the gap	61

EMPTINESS *by Nigel Wellings* — 77

A meditation on the pain of emptiness	81
A meditation on the delight of emptiness	95
Being present with emptiness	117
GLOSSARY	173
ENDNOTES	183
INDEX	187

LIST OF MEDITATIONS

PRESENT WITH SUFFERING IN LOSS AND BEREAVEMENT,
Elizabeth Wilde McCormick

- *Soften, allow and love*: Christopher Germer's meditation on compassion pp. 58–59
- *This moment, this only, all that there is*: A meditation from Amaravati Buddhist Monastery pp. 74–75

EMPTINESS, *Nigel Wellings*

- *A meditation on the empty self* pp. 97–99
- *Mindfulness of the breath* pp. 145–148
- *Mindfulness of emotions* pp. 155–157
- *'Doing nothing' meditations*: The basic practice, the 'Oxford' practice and a meditation from Pema Chödrön pp. 163–168

FOREWORD
by Henry Schukman

Robert Frost once said that a great poem is like an ice cube placed on a hot surface. It melts down upon itself, never shifting from its place. So the poem rests in and on its subject, and settles down into itself, until it is done.

Something analogous happens in Buddhist practice. The great mercy of Buddhism is that it places suffering at the centre. Nothing extraneous, nothing imaginary, nothing grand: just let's fully address suffering. It's a little like Chekhov said: that a story is fulfilled not when a problem is solved, but rather when it has been fully explored. So Buddhist practice invites us to fully explore suffering, our own and others', but generally starting with our own, until its origins have been clearly recognized, and its nature fully accepted.

The promise of this kind of practice runs something like this. Find your suffering, come to know it well and accept it, and compassion will naturally arise – the very compassion that melts the suffering from within. Suffering, rather than being the problem, is also in a sense the solution. If fully entered, embraced, allowed, above all through the practice of mindfulness, whereby we come to know it as sensations in the body, it becomes its own path of healing and awakening.

To many of us who have come to explore Buddhist-inspired practices, the possibility of addressing suffering – our own and others' – in this direct way, with the kinds of support and guidance the teachings encourage and offer, turns out to be a magnificent act of kindness. Rather than having to take on beliefs or sign up to unproven creeds that may exclude many, or wait for magical, other-worldly succor, the teachings reveal that to know what our pains, losses, hurts and agonies are, as actual phenomena in the here and now, without rejecting or resisting them, can not only marvelously reduce them, but also lead us to the kinds of liberation and 'realization' the traditions speak of.

Present with Suffering is a wise and compassionate book, a compelling double-act between two deep practitioners, both of them therapists and teachers, who have found solace and healing by looking into the last place we might want to look – namely our suffering itself. Through having thoroughly accepted their own hurts and griefs, they can speak from the depths of experience. Liz Wilde McCormick lost her beloved partner at a relatively young age, and the heartbreak that followed eventually turned, through her practice, into profound heart-opening. Nigel Wellings points us to the marvel of 'emptiness' as known in Mahayana Buddhism, that is the liberating treasure hidden within the pain of emotional 'emptiness', in which many of us may at times find ourselves stranded. Again, through non-rejection and non-resistance of that second kind of emptiness, namely the emptiness of distress and despair, and instead through allowing them, we can come to taste the boundless loving awareness that is a property of the other kind – Buddhism's miraculous 'emptiness.'

In the case of either approach, the isolation of emotional distress gradually opens to the healing power of connection. The frozen heart thaws and opens to others. Emptiness turns from solitary anguish to the liberative experience of boundless openness, which reveals a universal connectedness. The deep core of our being is touched into new life. And equally, in both cases, the entry to this renewal is through the pain of suffering itself, which both of these authors and trail-makers have gone through, and come to know intimately. They map their paths, and give us practices to point us along the deep, old ways they have found.

The pledge of Buddhism's first 'ennobling truth' is fulfilled here. Suffering exists; accept that, stoop under its lintel, rather

FOREWORD

than refuse it, and we find an endless path of healing opening before us.

This book is a welcome and treasurable guide to finding that path, and to following it. Deep suffering, grievous loss, traumas old and new, all take a heavy toll on our mental health. How we can grow through them, rather than deny or seek to avoid them, is the great gift offered here. Read and be restored, renewed. Follow the practices outlined here, and find the heart opened, healed and awakened.

Henry Shukman, author of *One Blade of Grass*,
Guiding Teacher, Mountain Cloud Zen Centre,
Santa Fe, New Mexico, 2022

ACKNOWLEDGEMENTS

Contemplating a subject such as suffering in loss and bereavement calls on many deep personal recollections and influences. I am grateful to have begun this conversation on suffering with my friend Jane Ryan while we were walking our dogs along the coast path in Suffolk. Conversations bring our thoughts into conscious awareness and become the building blocks for further thought and investigation.

Many, many people have contributed to my writing in this book. I celebrate my work as a psychotherapist for over forty years and am grateful to all patients and supervisees who have shared their own suffering. Before this, when I was a volunteer with the Samaritans I learned the most basic and precious skill of sitting, listening and sharing emotional pain. I am grateful to my early teachers in psychotherapy particularly: Dr Tony Ryle, Barbara Somers, Dr Nina Coltart. To my wonderful friends and colleagues, many of whom read some of the sections of this text: Margaret Landale, Linda Hartley, Dr Wasyl Nimenko, Dr Andy Harkin and Annalee Curran. Thanks to Linda Hartley for permission to include her somatic practice on page 53.

Grateful thanks to the Suffolk Coastal sangha for our weekly meditations and deep sharing which has been

ACKNOWLEDGEMENTS

consistent these last fifteen years. For my many retreats with Thich Nhat Hanh and the Plum Village community. For the writings of Thich Nhat Hanh, Pema Chodron and Dale Asrael. Many thanks also to Henry Shukman for taking the time to write the foreword.

I owe a debt of gratitude to Nigel Wellings, my long-term friend, colleague and co-author. While writing this text I was in considerable pain waiting for a hip operation and became exhausted, something he noticed and kindly named. Our sitting together and conversations returned me to basic practice. That in all aspects of suffering we start where we are, we begin by just sitting and creating a space, breath by breath. Once I had returned to what I have known, experienced and written about, but forgotten in the drive to complete something, I was able to ponder more deeply on the process of writing and galvanize more energy. Nigel took over the writing of the introduction and edited some of the earlier section and I am deeply grateful to him and his wife Philippa as we all shared in the process of creating this book.

Elizabeth Wilde McCormick

After a lifetime of psychotherapy and Buddhism my gratitude extends to a very long list of people – patients, students and teachers – who are seminal to what is written here. But

ACKNOWLEDGEMENTS

to keep it brief, first my wife Philippa Vick. We have always worked together, just about everything I write about here has come out of our collaboration. Furthermore, she has tolerated long hours of being an 'author's widow' while I wrote her inspirations down. In fact it is she who introduced me to the Zen teacher Henry Shukman who has very kindly written the foreword to this book. Though I was very pleased when he said yes it was only a little later when I read his astonishing book, *One Blade of Grass*, did I realize how very fortunate we were. Next, Liz McCormick – our friendship and fruitful working partnership goes back over twenty years. I was initially reluctant to write this book but when I actually got going I found it really enjoyable and am now grateful that her encouragement prevailed. The most difficult section for me was the Buddhist understanding of emptiness. Here several good friends researched and read through my attempts to make something enormously opaque readable to a non-Buddhist audience. Terry Pilchick, longstanding Buddhist practitioner and mindfulness teacher gently probed my philosophical understanding and Brendan McLoughlin, psychotherapist and owner of a mercurial brain, helped me through a deeper appreciation of Yogachara, an area of Buddhist philosophy I have often struggled with. Together we grappled with 'does the world actually exist beyond our perception?'. Once finished the piece was road tested by Clare Stent, Kay Cousins,

ACKNOWLEDGEMENTS

Hennie Symington and Penny Campbell. Each in their own way made valuable observations that found themselves incorporated into the text. Lastly my 'twin', being born on the same day and year, Jane Ryan who with Liz conceived of the whole project and Christina Wipf Perry and her team at Confer who got behind it. Thank you everyone.

Nigel Wellings

INTRODUCTION
by Nigel Wellings

*'Either way takes courage, either way wants you
to be nothing but that self that is no self at all'*

David Whyte

This book's beginning starts in the spring of 2019 with Liz, my long-time friend and colleague, and Jane Ryan, the founder of Confer, a provider of CPD events for therapists. Walking their dogs together along the Suffolk coast near where they live they fell into a conversation about their experiences of loss – something they both knew well – Liz's husband had died over twenty years before and Jane's more recently. By the end of the year this exchange had evolved into a conference hosted by Confer on the subject of *Being Present with Suffering*, during which both Liz and I were the speakers – Liz choosing to focus on bereavement and I on the different meanings of emptiness. From this came the invitation to write this book.

Life presents events we often have no control over. These events we then take and try to make sense of and those events that contain much pain may – at best – become invitations to engage with our life in a different way. As

INTRODUCTION

Liz says, 'Sometimes it is our experience of suffering that leads us to a deeper understanding about what it is to be human, and that we are all more than the sum of our parts.' Talking with Liz she reminds me that it was in 1992 that she went through a debilitating period of illness when suffering from meningitis. This led to her first encounter with the Buddhist monk and much-loved Vietnamese Zen teacher, Thich Nhat Hanh. Reading his books and beginning to attempt the meditation that he describes within them enabled her to find some stability and stillness – something that felt like a miracle at the time. From her illness came her initiation into being mindfully present with suffering.

Liz reminds us in her part of this book that suffering is inevitable and perhaps because of this we have all evolved our own and different ways of dealing with it. When we can find within the bleakness of our loss the possibility of something new then our grief, and all the past griefs that are carried within it, may be made more bearable. Recalling a conference she attended in 2012, in which the psychiatrist and psychotherapist Mark Epstein challenged the established beliefs about the process of bereavement, she releases us from the necessity of having any pre-identified sequence of emotions. Instead what is offered is the possibility of being with whatever our experience

INTRODUCTION

is, just as it is, for as long as it is. In this way grief may be allowed to take its own course and our relationship to it is to simply be present, perhaps consciously aware of our impermanence and the reality of the dying away and renewal that this implies. Here she draws upon the death of her husband John. As part of her grieving process a year later she visited Plum Village, a community that Thich Nhat Hanh had established in rural southern France after his expulsion from Vietnam following his political activism. Arriving there she describes her anxieties, that she would not fit in, that she would do it all wrong – fears derived from her childhood. However, what she in fact finds is an experience of coming home. Wrapped in love and acceptance by the community of practitioners, the *sangha*, her fears are dissolved. This second initiatory experience adds something to the first. We may be mindfully present with what hurts us but this is enormously strengthened when we have the support of others around us. This recognition of the part those close to us play in the experience of bereavement is a signature insight of Liz's writing here. Repeatedly she reminds us we cannot do it alone nor are we alone when we can open to others.

    For myself I cannot clearly say where this book began. I guess the problem is that once we begin to think in terms of emptiness – my subject within this book – we

INTRODUCTION

find there are no beginnings and ends within seamless change. However, there are themes and the two here are narrative and presence. These emerged in Liz's and my work together over twenty years ago while we were both newly appointed directors of training at the Centre for Transpersonal Psychology (CTP) in London. Prior to this the Centre's curriculum had been dominated by the Analytical Psychology of C. G. Jung and the Psychosynthesis of Roberto Assagioli, two systems of psychotherapy that particularly value making a meaningful narrative out of the unique events of a person's life and the centrality of the self. But now the Centre had been entrusted into our hands and we began doing something a little different, extending the curriculum to embrace new ideas from Transpersonal Psychologists in other parts of the world and, most importantly, introducing the practice of mindfulness.

Two books came out of this period. In 2000 Liz and I edited a collection of essays *Transpersonal Psychotherapy, Theory and Practice*, written by the Centre's new staff members. My own contribution was a chapter on psychopathology which drew upon Stephen Johnson's work found in his *Character Styles* and a second chapter, 'Naked Presence', that for the first time fully introduced into the Centre the work of the philosopher Ken Wilbur and the clinical psychologist John Welwood – two big names in the world of American

INTRODUCTION

Transpersonal Psychology. The evolution of both these chapters may be found in this book. Johnson's work remains a framework I use when trying to understand and describe the deep wounds that we carry from the earliest period of our life and the subsequent events that compound them. It is these we often meet when we let our meditation reach deeply down into ourselves and paradoxically it is working with these wounds that unfolds into spiritual awakening. But it is John Welwood's contribution that was particularly formative. In his seminal paper, *Reflection and Presence*, Welwood laid out a path of psychotherapy leading to and overlapping with Buddhist practice. A path that starts out with reflection upon our personal narrative and that leads, via being present with the felt-sense within our body, through mindfulness to non-dual contemplation. At this time, the discovery of this paper was a revelation. It laid out cogently the relationship between psychotherapy and Buddhism that I had myself been trying to formulate and, besides this, provided the scaffolding for CTP's new curriculum – an attempted marriage between a celebration of individual journey and the deeper insight that that there was no journey or anyone upon the path. It has also stood the test of time – this model continues to inform what I have written here.

The second book from this period was published in 2005 – *Nothing To Lose, Psychotherapy, Buddhism and*

INTRODUCTION

Living Life. It represents where Liz and I had reached by the end of our time with CTP. Continuing with the themes of narrative and presence we had taught along two parallel lines. One was the value of making meaning from the circumstances of our life, seeing life as an initiatory journey. A journey that it was important to have witnessed. The second was the necessity of being able to let go of our story when it becomes an impediment, causing more distress and confusion than it promised to resolve. As Zen would have it: 'dropping the self'. This perhaps needs some unpacking.

When we talk of personal narratives, the story of 'me' and my life, it is a two-sided blade. We are all beings who to be healthy depend upon making meaning out of our lives and when we cannot do so we may become both psychologically and physically ill. There is a deep, instinctive compulsion to do this – recall how in an instant we create an explanation for events that places them in some form of meaningful pattern. Those of us who are highly imaginative are particularly accomplished at this but even those who think themselves rational and down to earth do exactly the same albeit with less flourish! The activity of storymaking occurs on both conscious and unconscious levels. Most of us can readily tell a good listener about the highs and lows of our life and about the sort of person we believe ourselves to be. However, it is the unconscious story, the 'core beliefs' that we unknowingly harbour about ourselves that are, if anything, both more powerful and destructive. For instance the secret fear that I am unlovable or all on my own. The pervasive psychological sores left by trauma.

Another aspect of our personal story is that we defend it because when any element of it is questioned it feels threatening. Here again recall what it feels like when we are accused of being someone we feel we are not – outrage, resentment, hurt. Or the disruption when we lose something that feels integral to our being. My story of 'me' must on all accounts be protected because to not do so feels secretly like annihilation. And it is not just about me. We all hold conscious and unconscious stories about other people, other political beliefs, other countries, other genders and races. When these are fuelled by fear they quickly become discriminations in which the 'other' is cloaked in all sorts of fantasies, many of which are derived from those parts of our own disavowed personality: our projected violence, greed and stupidity. It is because of this dark side of our storymaking that it is a two-sided blade. Although we depend upon it for survival, it is simultaneously a deep source of misperception and the harm that stems from this. The stories I tell myself about

INTRODUCTION

myself and others can and do create great unhappiness and cruelty. And, deeper still, it is our stories that obscure knowing 'how things really are' – the Buddhist diagnosis of our continued discontent.

These profound shortcomings are in my part of this book challenged in section two by the Buddhist enquiry into self and perception, and in my third section by the slogans 'thoughts are not facts' and 'feels real, not necessarily true'. Both bring our automatic storytelling up short and by questioning it hope to exchange unconscious reactivity with a more considered – and kindly – responsiveness. They also open us to the liberating possibility of simply not knowing. The real pleasure and freedom of an empty space in which many more things are made possible. The relief of not having to be oneself. As my wife, Philippa Vick, says, once we have read the book, *All About Me and What I Think*, 50 times, the storyline is no longer griping.

So if that covers the good and bad angel of personal narratives, what about presence? Presence has become one of those words that have many meanings. Its roots go back to something concrete – it means being here, being at hand, being available in the present moment. Here it is used as a synonym for being mindful – another much abused word – cultivating a sustained, clear and relaxed awareness of what is happening within and around us

INTRODUCTION

in each consecutive moment. So we may be mindfully present which means we are present in a mindful way. Attentive, non-judgemental, curious, neither dissociated nor identified with the sensations, emotions and thoughts that arise within us.

When we bring mindful presence to our narrative – our story of what's going on – we see our story as no more than thinking. We step back. Mindfulness is the means to do this – we rest in the present moment and when we notice that we have been carried away by emotionally-laden thoughts we simply name this distraction 'thinking', let the thoughts go and return to the present. A movement away from the default setting of the mind to wander in the past and future towards present moment awareness. Mindfulness then is a training in not being seduced by the things we think and feel and this creates the possibility of choice. This is of fundamental value and for this reason Liz introduces it in her section on 'Mind the gap' and I then follow in my third section 'Being present with emptiness' with detailed instructions on how it is best practised.

One of the principle ways that this book uses the tool of presence is as a non-conceptual way to be with our emotions. Both Liz and I refer to being present with the 'felt-sense' – to be mindful of the emotions (and the meanings derived from them) in our bodies. When we

INTRODUCTION

are present with our emotions we just leave them as they are. We are not trying to explain or understand them, we are not trying to change or make them 'better' and we are certainly not trying to get rid of them. The premise is that they are fine already just as they are and if we can accept them, holding them mindfully and with kindness, they will naturally change of their own accord. What else could they do in a changing universe? It is only our fear and the contraction this causes that makes things appear to freeze and become stuck. This way of approaching things is the crux of the entire book. We do not pretend that painful thoughts and emotions can be 'cured' – that is, got rid of forever. They are part of being human, not an illness, but the real question is how can we be with this aspect of ourselves? How can we be with the things that hurt? Our answer is through awareness, acceptance, kindness and compassion – the components of wisdom.

By the time of the publication of *Nothing To Lose*, Liz and I had already started to take what we had learnt together out into the different areas of our lives. This was an amazingly fertile period. At the end of the 1990s psychoanalysis had discovered Buddhism and books like Mark Epstein's highly successful *Thoughts Without a Thinker* represented a rapprochement between the two previously antagonistic disciplines. Having first trained in

INTRODUCTION

Psychoanalytic Psychotherapy and then Jungian Analysis I now found myself returning to my first training as I realized its atheism sat more easily than the Jungian work that competed with Buddhism for the definitive spiritual vision. The psychoanalytic perspective seemed content to stay with the ordinary experiences of life whereas the Jungian, in its pursuit of 'individuation' now seemed to me somewhat narcissistic and hollow – plainly I had fallen out of love. Liz, for her part, was also on paths of new discovery during these years. Informed by her husband John's heart disease and her therapeutic work with heart patients in the cardiac department of Charing Cross Hospital that had begun in the mid-eighties, she continued, as a founder member of the Association for Cognitive Analytic Psychotherapy, to participate in its development. From this work came four books about the heart including her 'bestseller' *Change for the Better.* All this provided a wealth of experience that is here reflected in her section on the heart. In parallel, in 2001 Liz attended her first Pema Chödrön Buddhist retreat in America. Here I remember thinking her very brave as she set out for something she had no previous experience of so very far away. However, I misperceived her; more intrepid than I realized, in 2002 she travelled with a small group to visit Thich Nhat Hanh's root temple in Vietnam and

INTRODUCTION

then later with the group that accompanied Thich Nhat Hanh during his visit to China. And following this, in 2003, with my wife, attended one of the first Mindfulness Teacher Training courses run by Bangor University. An event none of us foresaw the implications of.

It is hard to imagine that in 2006 there were only a handful of books published on secular mindfulness. Now, I am told, there are hundreds of books or papers researching its efficacy published each week. During our transit from the Centre for Transpersonal Psychology, Liz, Philippa and I had created a group rather too grandly called The Forum for Contemplative Studies that met monthly to practise meditation and share the ideas that excited us. The inspiration for this had come from an American organization I had read about called Contemplative Mind in Society, which taught mindfulness within the spheres of the workplace, law, education and business – anticipating the secular mindfulness movement's dissemination of the practice. Provocatively they had also taught the staff at Monsanto – not known for being on the side of the angels even then – and the question had been asked: whether the practice of mindfulness carried the seeds of ethical behaviour and would infect its Monsanto practitioners for the good or would mindfulness simply be corrupted as it was used to make the morally bankrupt more efficient?

INTRODUCTION

Out of the Contemplative Forum grew the Bath and Bristol Mindfulness Courses, started by my wife Philippa Vick and then joined by myself several years later. This gets a mention here because the influence of the courses we taught and developed over the subsequent fourteen years is also present in this book and may be found especially in my section three, 'Being present with emptiness' which largely parallels the content of our joint teaching, a section that also answers the Monsanto question.

During this time Philippa and I gradually moved away from the combined Mindfulness-Based Stress Reduction (MBSR) and Mindfulness-Based Cognitive Therapy (MBCT) that was first taught by Bangor University towards something that relied more on the Buddhist sources that had been their inspiration. This showed particularly in the simplified mindfulness meditations we taught which were derived from the Insight Meditation Society, and the fact that we, as practising Buddhists, naturally infused our teaching with a Buddhist background. Many see this as a fault but I disagree – the power of mindfulness comes from its Buddhist source and if it were not for Buddhism its capitulation to neoliberalism and 'market forces' would have been even faster and more complete. That said, the core MBSR and MBCT courses have a great deal that is valuable in them and it continues to fascinate and amuse me that one of the first concepts within the MBCT course is 'automatic pilot', an idea that nearly all Buddhist philosophers have spent the last two-and-a-half thousand years wrestling with. This part of the journey is recorded in my book *Why Can't I Meditate, How to Keep Our Mindfulness Practice on Track*, published in 2015. Combining the shared insight of meditators, meditation teachers, my own learning and being very practical, it finds further expression throughout my part of this book.

Finally, it has been very interesting for me to see when writing this where Liz's and my own work has presently landed. Perhaps the biggest change is the inclusion of neuroscience. Both Liz and I mention the neurobiology of grief and trauma and it is largely from recent discoveries about these states of mind that modern trauma 'treatments', such as EMDR (Eye Movement Desensitization and Reprocessing), Somatic Experiencing and Sensory Motor Psychotherapy, now work from the body up, recognizing that the felt-sense is the key to being present with old hurts held within the coarse and subtle fabric of our body. As for Liz, she has more deeply cemented her practice of Vietnamese Zen that encompasses both Theravada and devotional Pure Land Buddhist influences. This very simple, emotionally warm and community-based Buddhism taught by Thich Nhat Hanh very much reflects the personality of my dear

INTRODUCTION

friend. She and her Suffolk Coast Sangha are present in the reoccurring note found in her writing that values the presence of others within community. People are dear and precious. For myself I have continued within the Nyingma tradition of Tibetan Buddhism that I first encountered in my mid-twenties – the mention of Dzogchen, the Great Perfection, as one form of non-dual Buddhist teaching alludes to the centrality of this in my life. Writing this book, it has actually surprised me how 'Buddhist' my writing has become and how the personal narrative aspect has seemingly fallen away. When a client recounts something to me now, my go-to response is not to ask how they feel about what they have just said but how were they with the emotions that were evoked. A question that invites presence to the narrative. Have I just become bored with myself with age? What is particularly heartwarming for me is that this relationship between psychotherapy and Buddhism that John Welwood articulated over 20 years ago has now been picked up and embraced by many meditation teachers and Buddhist psychotherapists. Established teachers such as Joseph Goldstein, Pema Chödrön, Tara Brach and my own Buddhist teacher Tsoknyi Rinpoche all mention or have very similar methods that help us remain present non-conceptually with what we experience within our bodies. Tsoknyi Rinpoche calls this the 'handshake

INTRODUCTION

practice' – making friends with our inner monsters – and it is identical in all but name. It seems like the day I was handed Welwood's paper on reflection and presence was one of the most important in my life.

And so we come to the end of the story – is it OK that it is a story? Of course it is, just as long as we remember it is all made up.

1

Present with Suffering in Loss and Bereavement

Elizabeth Wilde McCormick

Impermanence and attachment

PHILOSOPHY AND PSYCHOLOGY

There can be something of a paradox between our many varied human experiences of attachment and impermanence. Life brings both. There are times when we might cling onto our attachments as something solid that keeps us secure, times when we want things to stay the same. And yet within us everything is changing all of the time, our feelings and emotions, our body sensations, thoughts and attitudes, even the rhythm of our breathing. We are witness to the birth and death of the whole of nature with its seasons, both death and rebirth, often bringing in something new. Although the reality of impermanence can feel painful personally, its nature brings change and movement, essential for the growth of life.

Philosophy, psychology and religion have all created offerings for understanding and managing these two realities of living in a human body with emotions. Our longing and need for healthy attachment, particularly to a meaningful other, a group or a way of life are primarily biological and always strong. We are naturally social animals. Unlike most of the animal kingdom, we are born as helpless infants and cannot survive without a caring other. It is from these early years that our emotional development and capacity for social engagement is established as we develop and grow within a web of relationship with others – family, friends, neighbours, community, animals and plants, as well as ideas and beliefs. The more we have felt and internalized being securely held and loved simply for ourselves, however different we may be, and integrated this security within ourselves, the more resources we have to support us in our wrestle with change and loss, and with the reality of impermanence.

Loss associated with the death of a loved person, a partner, friend, family member, is always a shocking and painful experience. It sweeps us into a vast unknown as we face the challenge of living without the other. The more attached we have been to a person, the greater the overwhelming feeling when it can feel impossible to accept death as a part of life. We can feel blinded by loss, rail against our loss. We might cope by filling the empty space, become manically busy, throwing ourselves into work or another relationship; we might become depressed, sometimes with all the clinical markers – poor sleep, early waking – we give up our everyday rituals, don't bother to wash, stop talking, entertain gloomy thoughts.

But at any time of life, whatever our experience, it is

Impermanence and attachment

possible to develop the resources that allow us to stop and reflect. Then to open to being present with change and to the myriad of feelings and sensations this can bring.

All close relationships involve attachment and the loss of this is profound. It is when we have projected our desire and need for happiness on to others that we empty ourselves of our own agency and choice. Many of us will have phases in life when, for many different reasons, we become attached to an 'other', perhaps hoping that this object or person will fill the emptiness we feel and give us the security and happiness we crave. Alcohol, substances, food, money, relationships can all become objects upon which we are over-attached and dependent. We may live for a while in the illusion that it is this that keeps us happy, and we become terrified of losing it or doing without. But in doing so we lose our objective capacity to stand aside and reflect both cognitively and mindfully. It is when we can name and allow spaciousness around our craving and longing that we are able to really notice them, and our fears. We are then able to spend time with what has been our fear of emptiness and we begin to make a new relationship with our suffering. What once felt like raw emptiness becomes spaciousness.

There have been many different western psychological theories about patterns of human attachment that underpin behaviour and particularly responses to loss that have influenced social attitudes and medical or psychological treatment. In the late 1950s John Bowlby writes: 'Intimate attachments to other human beings are the hub around which a person's life revolves.'[1] He described four styles of attachment: secure; anxious and avoidant; anxious and resistant; and disorganized. He thought that people who have been able to develop secure attachment are likely to feel less empty than those with the other attachment experiences and are able to see others as supportive. Those who have learned and internalized the three other styles are less able to manage as well in the 'everyday' and negotiate the path of loss and grief. D.W. Winnicott described what he named the 'good enough mother' as not too good, not too bad, offering a 'facilitating environment'.[2] This combination he saw as able to help a growing child tolerate both positive and negative experiences and develop an ability to feel a 'true self'. For Winnicott, this is a sense of being alive and real in one's mind and body, having feelings that are spontaneous and unforced. This experience of aliveness is what allows people to be genuinely close to others, to be creative and also stand alone.

By the early 1970s, western psychology had begun to include other developments after psychoanalysis and behaviourism. Initially part of the humanistic movement, the 'transpersonal psychologies' became the fourth force in psychology. This allowed a space within psychological thinking that allows for states of mind beyond what was previously seen as 'normal' perception such as spiritual experiences, depth intuition, and contemplative and meditative practice. At its core is the understanding that human beings are capable of making a living and meaningful relationship with suffering.

There has been much concern in recent years about the pathologizing of 'ordinary' unhappiness such as responses to loss, and treating this as if it were a mental disorder needing medication. In the early 1980s, Cognitive Analytic Therapy (CAT) was developed at Guy's and St Thomas' hospitals in London in order to integrate the many theories from psychology and make a collaborative therapy available to many more people within the British National Health Service.[3] This approach to helping mental health suffering is also available in Europe, Australia and India. Dr Anthony Ryle, the pioneer of CAT, felt strongly about psychology's tendency to limit or pathologize human behaviour and not recognize that, given the opportunity, we all have the capacity for reflection, revision and trying something new, particularly when there is an established shared dialogue between two people, therapist and patient. He developed a therapy based upon a gathering and reframing of these well-researched ideas, freeing individuals to find their own voice whatever their presenting symptoms. This work allows for space to be created for the 'I' or ego to see the 'me' of original self to be revealed and find its voice. Through relational dialogue this therapy integrates different theoretical approaches to psychotherapy.

Within Buddhist thought, thousands of years older than modern psychology, we find another approach to the suffering from loss. The Vietnamese Zen Buddhist monk and teacher Thich Nhat Hanh teaches us that the first door of liberation from suffering is emptiness.[4] The emptiness here is not the Buddhist understanding of emptiness as the transitory and contingent nature of things, but the emptiness of form and goals, and that what we are so often looking for outside of ourselves is already here within us, but we cannot see it. This is our own capacity to stand aside from the content of our busy minds and become present with all that is – thoughts, feelings, sensations and ideas – compassionately and without judgement.

STAGES OF LIFE; STAGES OF GRIEF

Each stage of life celebrates this paradox of attachment and impermanence as a rite of passage – leaving the innocence of infancy and childhood and going to school; entering puberty, leaving home and entering the unknown outside world of work or marriage, forming a partnership and friendships, entering the work space. We may also have had to weather other changes such as our own illness, or illness within our family. Each stage of life is a birth of something new and each ending is a little death. The stages will not come again in the same way. Myriad forms of birth and death, large and small, dominate all animate life. Mark Epstein MD writes: 'One way or another death (and its cousins: old age, illness, accidents, separation and loss) hangs over us all. Nobody is immune.'[5]

The influence of psychological and medical responses to loss and bereavement has been considerable, particularly when grief becomes divided up into discrete stages like bus stops. Elisabeth Kübler-Ross worked with terminally ill patients in Switzerland in the 1960s and was one of the first doctors to write about death and dying.[6] She devised a template for the management of grief into five stages, pioneering at the time: denial, anger, bargaining, depression, acceptance; and stated that there is a point where one gets over it and reinvests the energy in a new relationship. At the time it was seen as a useful tool and became the norm for professionals helping those in grief. Now it seems to illustrate something about our western human fear of facing the reality of death and its aftermath and our need to feel in control. Later in the 1980s Dr Kübler-Ross ran workshops for carers and families with someone in the process of dying. Toward the end of her life and after being present at her mother's death she felt, like Dr Mark Epstein, that grief from loss actually never goes.

John Bowlby and his colleague Colin Murray Parkes described four stages of grief which reflect more on how our body and nervous system responds to grief:

- Shock and numbness within the physical body, feeling as if the loss is not real, or unable to be understood and accepted.
- Yearning and searching where we are still preoccupied with our loved one and with filling the void left by their presence.
- Despair and disorganization where, as we feel forced to accept that things have changed and cannot go back to how they were, we allow our more difficult feelings such as despair and anger to arise.
- Reorganization and recovery where our faith in life may start to come back as we start to rebuild and establish new goals, new patterns and new habits in life.

In his beautiful book called *The Wild Edge of Sorrow*, psychotherapist Francis Weller describes grief as not being just one thing but touches all aspects of our being and past experiences.[7] He describes five different gates that all of us will come up against at different times in our lives and in different

Impermanence and attachment

ways. Naming the gates allows us to reach into different parts of ourselves and our experience in a new way. The first gate will be familiar to anyone with a Buddhist approach to life: everything we love we will lose. Through the second gate we find those places within us that have not known love, places hidden away by shame or rejection we could call our unlived, unexplored life. The third gate takes us into connection with the sorrows of the world and the way in which they impact upon each of us. The fourth gate is interesting particularly for therapists, as it is that we expected but did not receive, such as our longing to belong, to be close and safe with the earth and others, to receive intimacy and closeness to another, to feel valued. We are often unaware of this gate until we experience grief from our current loss. And the fifth gate is ancestral grief, which we carry unconsciously in our bodies and minds from earlier generations.

There is an early Buddhist story that illustrates our human need for all the ingredients we have been addressing: the naming of our facing what feels like the impossibility of death, support for shock from listening others, an attempt at action and finally understanding after the death of a loved one.

During Buddha's time, a woman named Kisa Gotami married young and gave birth to a son. One day, the baby fell sick and died soon after. Kisa Gotami loved her son greatly and refused to believe that her son was dead. She carried her son's body around her village, asking if there was anyone who could bring her son back to life. The villagers all saw that the son was already dead and there was nothing that could be done. They advised her to accept his death and make arrangements for the funeral. In great grief, she fell upon her knees and clutched her son's body close to her. She kept asking her son to wake up. A village elder took pity on her and suggested she consult the Buddha: 'Kisa Gotami we cannot help you but you should go to the Buddha, maybe he can bring your son back to life!' Kisa Gotami was extremely excited upon hearing the elder's words. She immediately went to the Buddha's residence and pleaded with him to bring her son back to life. The Buddha replied, 'Kisa Gotami, I have a way to bring your son back to life.' 'My Lord, I will do anything to bring my son back.' 'If that is the case, then I need you to find me something. Bring me a mustard seed, but it must be taken from a house where no one residing in the house has ever lost a family member. Bring this seed back to me and your son will come back to life.' Having great faith in the Buddha's promise, Kisa Gotami went from house to house, trying to find the mustard seed. At the first house, a young woman offered to give her some mustard seeds. But when Kisa Gotami asked if she had ever lost a family member to death, the young women said her grandmother died a few months ago. Kisa Gotami thanked the young woman and explained why the mustard seeds did not fulfil the Buddha's requirements. She kept moving from house to house but the answer was always the same – every house had lost a family member to death. Kisa Gotami finally came to realize that there is no one in the world who has never lost a family member to death. She now understood that death is inevitable and a natural part of life. Putting aside her grief, she buried her son in the forest. She then returned to the Buddha and became his follower.[8]

This ancient story illustrates the initial incomprehension and disbelief in the shock of a young death followed by a search for something that would offer support to the feelings of helplessness. The action of going to each house and speaking about death with others brings Kisa Gotami into touch with others until she realizes the shared fact of death. Only then is she able to take the reality inside herself, return to the source of the ritual and follow a new path.

THE CHALLENGE OF GRIEF TO OUR WHOLE BEING

Grief makes us feel unsafe – whatever attachment has gone before, whether to an idea, a place, a job, a friend or lover, has been torn away, sometimes brutally as in sudden or mysterious death or suicide. What might have been our safe haven with another is no longer. We are exposed, and in shock. Grief can make us feel as if we are totally alone in the world, a frightening feeling for humans with their need for social engagement. Numbness can offer protection ... but most often our initial experience is that there are no words for our experience, no words for feelings, fear, anxiety, loss of sense of self.

We may manage apparently well and then sometime later fall apart at something that appears quite small – someone shouts at us in the bank, we cannot find a tin opener, we get lost travelling to a familiar destination. But this apparently small event can be the trigger that allows feelings to arise. Then we have an opportunity to notice, respect, record and share with a trusted other. When our feelings can find words, we have the opportunity to be released from the hold of our emotions that have been held in the body.

Loss through death of a close person challenges all our previous thinking and beliefs, it takes us into new territory emotionally. We need close others and community to offer support and comfort. This recognition, particularly from known, loved and respected others means we are less alone. Family and friend support, good neighbours, a spiritual belief about change, loss, death, impermanence, community rituals such as flowers, notes, prayers, chanting, singing together are vital sources of nourishment. This natural environmental and familial support often means that people are able to grieve freely in whatever way they are able, and to follow the course of bereavement without becoming pathologically overwhelmed and in need of medical or psychological treatment or the support of psychotherapy.

Throughout the world, different cultures offer very varied ceremonies and rituals for death according to their beliefs and needs, from the Sky burials in Mongolia and Tibet to the culture still in some villages in Italy and Spain where it is the norm to wear black for at least a year, signifying a person engaged in the mourning process. It can also be viewed as a way of granting permission to be quiet, to not have to make effort, their suffering automatically recognized and respected.

Losses that are sudden, unexpected, violent – those lost at sea, burnt in fires, the death of a child, death from suicide which leaves so many questions and anguish – can create such shock that cutting off feeling is initially the only response available and an important protection. Loss through death may also touch on earlier wounds of loss. Frances Wellers' description of the five gates offers us a useful understanding. He names the second and fourth gates as places where we have had earlier experiences of loss due to neglect, abuse and disinterest. This is particularly intense in early life when we have no means of understanding our loss which is then carried by our body as an early traumatic wound. These earlier experiences will be reawakened and may compound the complexity of our feelings. Such events and experiences can become buried for years, perhaps only surfacing after being triggered by another bereavement and perhaps when it's possible to address the earlier trauma of loss and for a grieving process to begin. It is never too late! In the next part we will be looking at how the trauma of loss can be carried in the body, expressing itself in different ways.

In September 2012 I attended a two-day series of talks between the Buddhist teachers and psychotherapists Jack Kornfield and Mark Epstein in New York. It was a spontaneous conversational affair, and they embarked on a dialogue about grief, bringing back their overnight reflections on the second day that was a valuable insight into the benefits of mindfulness. When Mark Epstein said, 'Grief never goes' there was a gasp from the five or six hundred people listening. They both reflected on the myriad ways we might be invited into coping with the death of a loved one. Mark Epstein (Epstein and Kornfield, 2012) reflects on the ways medicine and psychology have attempted to divide grief into phases and says:

> There is no authority on grief and that whilst nothing stays the same that does not stop things being as

they are. Grieving should be allowed to go on forever and the practice of mindfulness is to relate to grief and hold in mind the experience of grief. We hold in the field of awareness the unbearable truth of impermanence.

Talk by Jack Kornfield and Mark Epstein at the Centre for Ethical studies, New York September 2012.

MINDFULNESS

The practice of mindfulness was taught by the Buddha almost two and a half thousand years ago. This practice offers us a way to remain present with our experience, without changing it or judging it, in each consecutive moment. Mindfulness cultivates equanimity – whether we are feeling loving or compassionate, angry, frightened or stuck, all mental states are received within an attitude of *maitri*, a Sanskrit word that may be translated as loving kindness or unconditional friendliness. It is the cultivation of mindfulness that can be seen as a gift that allows us to choose how to be with the impact of our suffering. For instance, when the pain of the death of a beloved person is compounded by our previous emotional wounds, this is what Cognitive Analytic Therapy describes as our 'core emotional pain'. What helps us to befriend our core pain is to recognize it and give it space, to be present with it mindfully. It also helps to be among and practise alongside others who understand and accept the challenges and vulnerabilities of being human.

The Vietnamese Zen Buddhist monk, Thich Nhat Hanh, teaches that, of the Three Jewels of Buddhism – the Buddha, the Dharma and the Sangha – the most important of these is the Sangha, the community of practitioners. This is a gathering of laity and monastics who practise the Buddha's teachings together, generating a shared field of mindfulness. Thich Nhat Hanh is particularly associated with Engaged Buddhism. This perspective emerged during the war between the nationalist Viet Minh and the French colonial government, which ended in 1954. From this period on, Engaged Buddhism, which sought to apply Buddhist teaching and practice to the suffering caused by war, social injustice, and political oppression, became more internationally known. However, in Vietnam, the communist government gradually came to perceive this as a threat and, in 1966, Thich Nhat Hanh, as an energetic exponent of Engaged Buddhism, was expelled from his country for his activism while attending a peace conference concerning the Vietnam war. Now, no longer able to return to his home, he and his monastic group built a monastic community near Bergerac called Plum Village and continued to practise in France. Today his teachings are practised by communities dedicated to his teachings all over the world.

Impermanence and attachment

In 2000, on the first anniversary of my husband John's death, I travelled to Plum Village. I had been following Thich Nhat Hanh's teaching and sitting with his mindfulness practices since 1992 when I was recovering from meningitis. It was truly wonderful to enter this community and the sense of peace and spaciousness it invited as well as the kindness in the smiles, the voices and the singing. And, as with all new experiences, our fears and vulnerability travel with us! The first morning when I joined the community for the 5 a.m. meditation I noticed many familiar fears arising – that I would not fit in, that I would not be good enough, I was only a beginner meditator and I might get it wrong. I might cough or fart in the silence and be chastised. But the opposite happened. I sat along with the monastics on my first morning at the 5 a.m. meditation and when the uncomfortable thoughts arose, and I continued to concentrate on the inbreath and outbreath, I experienced physically the energy of collective silent loving kindness from all the monastics sitting behind me in the meditation hall. Tears poured down my face. It was a profound experience of receiving unconditional love and kindness for which I will always be grateful. It was a huge welcoming embrace at the beginning of my regular practice and joining a sangha in the UK. That collective great heart began to heal my own wounded heart.

PRESENT WITH SUFFERING

Just before I left Plum Village, I was given this breath poem written by Sister True Virtue which I read often and share with many who have lost loved ones. Each line is read with one breath:

No coming no going
No after no before
I hold you close to me
I release you to be free
Because I am in you
And you are in me.

The human body in loss and bereavement

> *Grief has no distance, grief comes in waves, paroxysms, sudden apprehensions that weaken the knees and blind the eyes and obliterate the dailiness of life.*
>
> Joan Didion 2005[9]

In a rational world it is often hard to comprehend that it is our non-verbal body that takes the immediate strain of loss as part of our coping mechanism. The body is our prime container for feelings and sensations. It is the vehicle through which we become conscious and aware of the many forms of stimuli and their effect, particularly our thoughts. All losses and the process of grief and bereavement that follow involve our physical body and nervous system. We are in a state of shock; rather than opening outwards to receive, our senses close down to try to protect us and our energy. This process is important during shock, for it protects us from a flood of painful feelings until we are able to find ways to be with them more consciously. It also protects us from extra stimulation at a time when we have few resources. But the loss of our senses as reminders of self-care can mean that we are not in touch with what we need: we can forget to eat, we often cannot rest or sleep, our joints and muscles ache, our skin feels deprived of touch, it's harder to see colour or receive the sound of music in a way we may have known as nourishing. It can be hard to breathe, and hard to stop, to allow any gap and get any rest. We may feel numb or as if we have the flu. Our thoughts might be dominant, going over and over what has happened. If it is our default position, we may feel driven to keep busy 'doing' rather than just 'being', arranging all the business surrounding our loss particularly after death, registration, burial, letters and information. We may move into automatic, experience numbness and disorganized thinking, disbelief at the death, whether this has been anticipated or not. It's as if we have lost our familiar light and are in the dark.

The physical aspects of bereavement need holding. Within ourselves and with others, a hurt body needs comfort; all experiences of loss require connection with others in an open and kind way. If we remain unaware of the impact on our body during these times, our energy becomes depleted and exhaustion quickly follows. In many western cultures those suffering loss through death of a loved one are often encouraged to carry on with all their daily activities, to put a brave face on it despite what they may be feeling and suffering. This is often admired and congratulated. Sometimes it can feel as if

The human body in loss and bereavement

there is no permission or support to stop in order to allow moments of safe spaciousness so that feelings and sensations might be noticed and cared for. This can make us feel very alone. There may be great pressure to 'get through it all' as if there were another side to go to without death being part of life and any sorrows would all be over. In cultures where an understanding that death is part of life exists, there are well-developed rituals for loss, and a support network of friends, family and community who share an understanding of the need to stop, rest, reflect and receive at these times of depletion. Grief is held kindly until the person is ready for the outside world again. These ancient rituals of comforting the bereaved often include touch, rocking, the smell of oils and incense, holding and a deep respect. All this is nourishment for the senses. They also help to develop a connection to a collective compassionate heart nourished by the rituals of compassionate beings.

As we saw in the last chapter, some of the early pioneers of naming the process of bereavement in stages hoped to create something solid, as if grief were a series of defined stepping stones that we need to work through in order to get over it. This can create considerable pressure, and it can be hard to take the time we need to gradually allow awareness of the senses of the body and the information they offer to awaken. Also, when the many gaps created by loss feel so empty and full of painful feelings, it's hard to stop and pause and reflect, to find what we and our body really need.

Finding a safe way to access a helpful reflective pause is so important to human well-being on all levels. Learning to be present with the pause and allowing ourselves to find comfort and support from the touch and warmth of others are some of the stepping stones needed for release. In this Covid year when so many of us have been forced to stop and be in one place, often our homes, there have been many stories of people noticing and being nourished by birdsong, flowers growing, the clean air and silence from aircraft and the kindness of strangers. It's as if our senses have had an opportunity to open. There are stories of how these experiences have brought people into a new relationship with their bodies, their senses and relationships. Alongside this, we are witnessing death throughout the world, the plight of those seriously ill in hospital and much physical and psychological suffering. Those who have lost loved ones to Covid have been unable to be with their loved ones as they lay dying, and later, after death, to be together in shared ritual, depriving them of the much needed physical sharing. The same is so in care homes with so many people deprived of touch and holding. Many elderly people have been rendered speechless by the loss of physical contact.

Dr Jane Buckle, PhD, RGN, creator of the 'M' Technique and author of numerous published articles about touch over the last 25 years has researched the effects of touch in both the USA and the UK. In conversation, she says:

> Touch and smell are possibly our most important senses, which is why babies develop them in the womb. However, whereas some people can manage when they lose their sense of smell, people deprived of touch can suffer from acute 'skin hunger'. In loss and bereavement, touch plays a vital role, helping reconnect a person to themselves, as well as the world around them. Gentle touch in bereavement and loss can allow a person to open up and share their feelings, often for the first time. This opening up can be the start of healing. As a nurse, I was privileged to share those intimate moments of someone's grief, patient or relative. Touch doesn't need words. It can be enough just to know someone cares and is there for you.
>
> In conversation with myself for this book.

TRAUMATIC LOSSES

When a violent or unexpected death occurs, our nervous systems are plunged into crisis and we often enter a world of unknown forces. It can be terrifying. Death due to suicide is always hugely shocking and can feel like complete rejection of relationships as well as of life, and, whatever the reasons that might be offered for taking one's own life, suicide leaves many never-to-be-answered questions and opens old wounds. We may also have to suffer police or legal investigations and enter worlds that we may know little about. This makes our grief and the bereavement process complicated and extended, sometimes for always.

Many of the soldiers returning from the First World War were so traumatized by their experience that they never spoke of it but sat, often numbed and silent, unable to respond or return to the life they had before. We now know that 'shell shock' is not something to be seen as cowardice but understand how post-traumatic stress affects the body and nervous system and fortunately there is much more help for soldiers. US soldiers returning from Vietnam in 1975, wounded after witnessing traumatic deaths within both their own group and Vietnamese families, had to carry this suffering alone. Many of them fled into the forests unable to return to their previous lives. The US forces lost 58,000 men in the 20 years of fighting in Vietnam and many, many more Vietnamese died. But there was little or no support within healthcare services for the returning soldiers with post-traumatic stress disorder (PTSD), all of them trained to deny the body senses in order to be soldiers, many of them brainwashed to carry on regardless of conflict and violence. They had no resources for the damage to their nervous systems.

The human body in loss and bereavement

Since the war ended in 1975 it is estimated that approximately 60,000 veterans have taken their own lives. Violent death takes a huge toll on the surviving human beings, particularly when attitudes to the human body were based on denial of fragility.

The geography of Vietnam and its people still carry the multiple scars of this war. In his book *At Hell's Gate*, Claude Thomas, who served as a soldier during the Vietnam war and is now a Zen monk and peace activist, writes about his raw feelings being triggered on his return to Vietnam when he saw his old enemy and his old enemy saw him.[10]

> *When I placed my awareness on my breath, I became more and more rooted in the present moment and was able to be in direct contact with my suffering, so it did not control me. I did not have to act out my suffering through violence or aggression.*

Based on the teaching of Thich Nhat Hanh, this core practice at Plum Village is a powerful means of being mindfully present with the breath. From the *Satipatthana Sutta*:

> *Breathing in, I know I am breathing in*
> *Breathing out, I know I am breathing out*
> *In, out.*

PRESENT WITH SUFFERING

WHEN DEATH OPENS EARLIER TRAUMA

All life events involving loss will touch the wounds of earlier losses that the body remembers. These wounds may not have been conscious, particularly if they were created in early life and never named or expressed but buried for the purpose of survival. We have seen that in Frances Weller's work he names two of the gates as being the loss of being unloved and cared for, and the losses carried by our ancestors but never recognized. For leading world trauma scientist Bessel Van der Kolk, the body does not lie and keeps the score.[11] In understanding that it is the body that leads the way throughout our lives, communicating to us through our posture, symptoms, energy and breathing, we are invited to bring into conscious awareness and name what our bodies have carried, step by step, and have the opportunity to heal whatever have been our earlier trauma and loss. In the conclusion to *Traumatic Stress*, Bessel Van der Kolk writes:

> The paradox is that in the process of accepting the reality of trauma, it is easy to lose one's sensitivity and to retreat into dry scientific observation or cynical capitulation. However, beneath the tidiness of emotional distancing and scientific classification lie the human vitality and energy to struggle against, and

create meaning out of, what appears to be the random cruelty of fate. This struggle to transcend the effects of trauma is among the noblest aspects of human history.[12]

Whatever the nature of the death of our loved person, if we have experienced earlier traumas such as being abandoned, harmed, abused as a child or adolescent, we are plunged back into the past memories, often through our bodies. All early trauma survivors feel as if they are permanently on alert. Their nervous systems are overactive, dissociation has helped them survive horrible events, but loss, particularly through death, often triggers earlier events through flashbacks. The needed bereavement process for that which has been lost, in some cases a happy childhood or feeling valued and loved, has had to be suspended, 'on hold', and not named. This is only available when there is safety with others, when a feeling of real acceptance has occurred. Much of the work of therapy with trauma and complex trauma is to give safe enough space for the bereavement process on many different levels to be allowed safely. The mourning process needed is usually related to loss of innocence and childhood, loss of safety, loss of a sense of self and real difficulty in accepting help or kindness because of its association with difficult feelings such as shame. One person I worked with realized during her therapy that she had become almost phobic about receiving any form of kindness, which made it doubly difficult for her to offer kindness to herself and her wound of sexual abuse. For her, kindness had been used as a way of seducing and grooming prior to abuse. She found the courage to realize and name this, which was the beginning of healing as she dared to tolerate receiving support. She was extraordinarily kind to others but had to spend many years learning to allow and constantly remind herself to be kind to herself, a core practice in being present, moment by moment. There's a need to tell the long buried story of what has happened to us, and what we lost, slowly, so that it is grounded in reality, acknowledged, believed and witnessed by others.

In the last 20 years the Sensorimotor Psychotherapy Institute in the USA has pioneered therapeutic work with trauma following all the studies in neuroscience in recent years.[13] They have developed a map showing how we can become dysregulated by our survival patterns and need to find a 'window of tolerance' where it feels safe enough to have a pause amid the constant vigilance or shutdown created by our traumatized body's needs. Our natural nervous system response to threat is fight or flight, which can include speeded up thinking, over-busyness, running away, avoiding in order to find safety and to feel in control. We can fight the idea of death through our anger and rage, our protest, and we can run away into thoughts or actions. The opposite occurs when we are overwhelmed by overarousal, and our nervous system shuts down into freeze, flag or faint. The freeze response in the early stages of loss is usually prevalent and protective. We cannot think, about the event, the person. Often, we need to be told over and over the details of what has happened.

These five nervous system responses are protective mechanisms for our need for safety. We can learn to recognize which one we are in, name it, and allow this recognition to support our finding our own 'window of tolerance' where we can begin to find a more comfortable connection with our bodies and discover the feelings our body carries and their felt sense. Ultimately this process helps us to be able to reflect and process what has happened to us.

A stark illustration of this is from someone who came to see me suffering from repeated nightmares following the death of his father. When he was telling me about his experience of being beaten at boarding school when still very young, he sat upright, very still and spoke like an automaton, his teeth clenched, his hands grasping the chair. His eyes looked dull and fixed. I asked him what he was experiencing, and he shrugged and, without engaging or stopping to reflect, said, 'It never did me any harm'. He had no language with which to join the general community of other boys other than removing himself from any feeling expression but soldiering on without feeling. He was experiencing this once again through nightmares, bringing into conscious awareness this early suffering at the same time as the loss of his father. This armour, so well developed, became our starting place for exploration and a safety net he could return to if his feelings became overwhelming. When I invited him to write a letter as if he were the armour, he surprised himself by writing, 'I am so tired. I just carry on. On automatic. Nothing gets through.' Later I asked him if he felt the armour had done the work needed but was needed no longer, he pondered on it and wrote, 'I really want a proper hug.' As he read out the letter, speaking from his armour, he wept. What had been forced out by the survival were memories of the warm cuddles with his grandmother. Their cuddles had to remain secret from his stern father who was determined 'to make a man of me'. In contacting her memory, bringing in photographs, he gradually befriended the young boy who had found real solace at his grandmother's house. When I asked what his father might have made of him choosing to have some therapy he winced. 'Therapy's just for wimps. Wimps.' This young man even found some humour around this memory saying, 'If he could see me now, here in the room! Doing this …' His body had softened, he was able to find the subtle movements of relaxation and humour. His nightmares ceased.

The human body in loss and bereavement

THE HUMAN FUNCTION CURVE

Fatigue and exhaustion are part of the early experience of loss and grief where, if we are protected from having to make too many decisions or take part in too many activities, we may find rest and connection with our loved one by engaging with memory, photographs, reading, music. If we can find enough rest and, ultimately, stillness within rest, we are able to listen and engage with more of the language expressed through our bodies. This can help lead the way for us to grow something of an unconditional presence with all our experience, just as it is, without judgement or over-attachment.

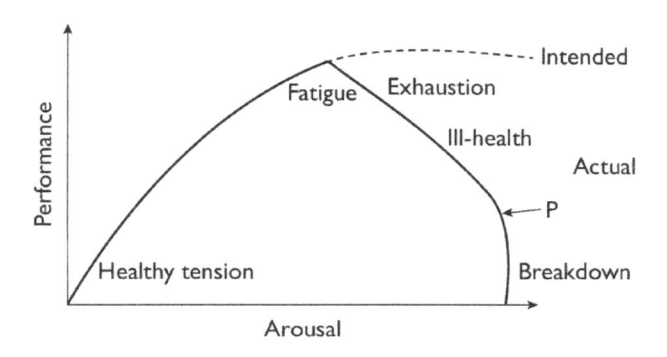

P – the point at which even minimal arousal may precipitate a breakdown

Adapted from Dr P.G.F. Nixon's paper – 'We all need Homeostasis'

PRESENT WITH SUFFERING

The Human Function Curve was developed in 1946 to help soldiers returning from battle recognize their levels of exhaustion and to measure their recovery. This map is also used at the Institute of Heart Math in Colorado and was introduced to me during my time at Charing Cross Hospital, and I have used it with many patients.[14] The graph illustrates the upward curve of healthy body and nervous system arousal, which increases as more is demanded, and how up to a point the increasing arousal helps us deliver more action. But as we reach the peak of what we can achieve, the P point on the diagram, we experience tiredness and the need to withdraw, rest and recover. The healthy response to tiredness is to stop, restore energy levels through rest, play and sleep and so return to the start of the graph, and to be able to accomplish this on a regular basis. But those of us who, through temperament, life situation or lack of recognition especially after bereavement, do not know how to recognize fatigue or are too afraid to stop may continue on down the downslope of the curve. As we continue trying to close the gap between our intended action and what is actually happening as we get more and more tired and our energy is dropping, our anxiety and fatigue are increasing, our attempts to complete tasks failing. Unable to rest or sleep we approach burnout and collapse. It then takes one small event to trigger a breakdown point. Sometimes this breakdown point is triggered by something relatively small and we just collapse. Sometimes it is when we feel let down because others do not understand and criticize us for our failings. Sometimes it is when people avoid speaking to us because we are so involved, head down, on the treadmill of just surviving.

The breakdown point is an important one. We can see it positively, as if our body has 'kept the score' and says 'no'. It can be a time when our body has granted us permission to stop, to rest, to be taken care of, to find the nourishment and help we long for. This can be hard! It is a time when our deeper feelings can arise, perhaps very painfully at first.

In my work with breakdown, I draw another half circle under the bottom line to include two other phases: thawing out and rebuilding.[15] We need time to repair and reflect, to begin to put things into perspective. In thawing out, we begin to feel in touch with the intensity of our emotional and physical pain, and it's a time to weep and rage as we experience darkness and enter a period of waiting. As T. S. Eliot writes in his poem *East Coker* 'The faith and the hope and the love are all in the waiting'.[16] I call this 'active waiting' for we are in a time where nothing is quite clear: we need to find safe spaces for this time to reveal what we need most in our bereavement process, for at first it is often not distinct. We need kind others to support and hold us and all the rituals of kindness we can find. We need to take time to learn to

PRESENT WITH SUFFERING

nourish our heart space and what it might reveal. We can use the image of the 'energy bank' to reflect on how much energy there might be within us. If we ask this question, usually, our body will have an answer! – 50 per cent, 40 per cent, 10 per cent. If there is only 30 per cent how might we use this in our day? My own experience of this is that I learned after my own bereavement that I could only do three different things in each day and needed to choose what they were.

What helps throughout these times is to develop real awareness of our breathing. We can celebrate each breath as we sit, walk, lie. As we follow the breath down through the chest area, we can imagine dropping down into the heart space. Here we learn to rest easy, to be able to enter into moments of stillness, however small. It is in the heart space that we register the return of our playful feelings, our joy, freedom and, also, times when we are lonely, angry, overwhelmed.

After thawing out we can enter a phase of rebuilding our strengths, old and new, perhaps a stronger sense of ourselves and we may enter the world more on our new terms. We still carry the memory and love of our loved ones in our hearts and perhaps learn to hear their voices in a helpful way, to invite them to walk alongside us. We enter life with a more awakened presence.

The practice of walking mindfully also helps us remain present with our body. As we walk, we touch the earth with our feet, we can also breathe in and out of the earth herself. We can feel a connection with the earth and all her qualities with each breath. We can go one breath, one step at a time. From Plum Village:

I have arrived
I am home
In the here
In the now
I am solid
I am free
In the ultimate I dwell

Heart

Give sorrow words, the grief that does not speak
whispers o'er the fraught heart, and bids it break.
                                    Macbeth, Shakespeare

The heart is a profound image for most people. I have devoted this section to matters relating to the heart because so many people refer to their heart when speaking about their suffering in relation to loss and bereavement. This is particularly so after the death of a loved person as the chest area or heart space is often referred to as the place that carries our physical manifestation of grief, a gathering place for feeling, sensations and memories. Described is a heavy heart, a stone in the heart and a broken heart. There is often a need to touch the space around the heart with tenderness. It is a wonderful starting place for mindful reflection and for the development of spaciousness and healing around the wound of loss.

There is a heart that is not seen when surgeons open the chest. I call this the invisible 'feeling heart' that resonates inside us all the time.[17] Completely different from but interwoven with the pump of the 'worker heart', the feeling heart, with its precise poetic language, takes us directly into our intimate inner life, our psychology, hopes, fears and aspirations.

How we experience and respond to our feeling heart has implications for our worker heart. Medical research throughout Europe and the USA since the 1980s shows that unacknowledged long-term anxiety and depression, unacknowledged anger and hostility can affect the worker heart and contribute to heart disease. Giving space for images and feelings generated in the heart area means allowing ourselves to find words for feelings and give them a voice. This may allow us to listen mindfully to what our heart tells us, and learn to give a heartfelt compassionate attention to our experience, for the experience of grief does not follow logic or any path we have previously travelled.

In *The Wild Edge of Sorrow* Francis Weller writes:

> It is the accumulated losses of a lifetime that slowly weigh us down – the times of rejection, moments of isolation, when we felt cut off from the sustaining touch of comfort and love. It is an ache that resides in the heart, the faint echo calling us back to the times of loss. We are called back, not so much to make things right but to acknowledge what has happened to us. Grief asks that we honour the loss, and in so doing honour our capacity for compassion. When grief remains unexpressed it hardens, becomes as

solid as a stone … When we are in touch with all of our emotions, we are more verb than noun, more a movement than a thing. But when our grief stagnates, we become fixed in place, unable to move and dance with the flow of life. Grief is part of the dance.[18]

For many years the organ of the heart was seen as a 'no go' area for surgeons. But since William Harvey's discovery in 1628 of the heart as a pump for blood to circulate and give us a pulse, modern cardiology has grown and developed significantly. In 1967 Dr Christian Barnard performed the first heart transplantation, and surgery on the heart continues to develop and expand. There are now numerous ways of repairing the pump and vessels of the heart when they have become diseased. It can now be micromanaged by modern equipment, taken out, cut, given electric shocks, stitched with vessels to replace old worn arteries as well as replaced by the heart of another. As cardiology has grown and developed, the interest in and understanding of the heart as a vehicle for feeling and imagination has fallen away.

It has fallen to modern reflective depth psychology, in particular the contribution of C. G. Jung and James Hillman, to remind us of the heart that has always been held by our poetic imagination. Jung writes: 'We may know, in the head, something for forty years, but it is not until it has touched us in the heart that we really take notice of it.' We speak easily in many languages of the lionheart of courage, the heart stirred by beauty; the heart broken by despair and loss, the heart touched and opened by love. In Spanish, the word for remember, 'recordar', translated literally, means 'to bring again through the heart'.

In his Eranos lectures printed in Spring Publications in 1981, James Hillman speaks of Henry Corbins' work of 1969 where he writes:

> This power of the heart is what is specifically designated by the word *himma*, a word whose content is perhaps best suggested by the Greek word enthymesis, which signifies the act of meditating, conceiving. imagining, projecting, ardently desiring – in other words, of having (something) present in the thymos, which is vital force, soul, heart, intention, thought, desire …
>
> (CI: 224)

In his work *The Thought of the Heart*, Hillman invites us to ponder on the human journey of soul making.[19] Soul is used here as a description of the ways in which we may deepen event into experience, where we embrace gladly in welcome, and fluidly, the varieties of human emotion rather than turning them into something solid.

Heart

The Institute of Heart Math is continuing with these explorations by researching both the organ of the body and shared human experience.[20] They have discovered that there is a little brain in the heart containing 40,000 neurons which sends more information to the brain than the brain does to the heart. In this new field of neurocardiology scientists have discovered that the heart possesses its own intrinsic nervous system – a network of nerves so functionally sophisticated as to earn the description of a 'heart brain'. This 'little brain in the heart' gives the heart the ability to independently sense, process information, make decisions, and even to demonstrate a type of learning and memory. Their research also shows that when two people sit together with peaceful intention and truly present to each other, listening, we might say with a good heart, there is cardiac coherence, and attunement – this has now taken its place as a reality, not just a psychological theory.

There are also recent studies in embryology showing that a group of cells at the top of the gestating embryo are already destined to become the heart, and they descend as early as four weeks of gestation into the centre of the body, forming this little brain in the heart. Whenever we notice within ourselves a call from our heart in whatever form or hear the words 'my heart is breaking', 'my heart is full of longing for what has been lost', we might reflect on this natural intelligence of the heart and allow it to lead the way.

James Lynch describes the medical consequences of loneliness, when people become cut off from the heart of family, familiar communities or systems of meaning.[21] As well as depression, it is the physical heart that suffers. During the lockdowns in our current coronavirus pandemic, individual experiences of loneliness have increased. Suffering has been acute when the heart has not been nourished by the warmth of friendly voices, by touches of kindness or by being free to share in the energy of friendship.

In the rush of modern life, with its pressure on achievement, keeping busy, carrying on whatever we are feeling, the heart as organ, image and metaphor can become overlooked and its value negated. Many professionals working in our British health service feel as if they are trying to 'close the gap' particularly in the mental health system, and particularly in the years of Covid-19. They are being asked to do more and more in less and less time against greater odds and often for less money and security. This is a perfect description of Type A behaviour first described and researched by Rosenmann and Freidman in the 1980s as a risk for heart disease.[22]

If our collective working environment has lost heart and become sick at heart, we can feel isolated and under threat. Stress is not just created by overwork, it is created by defeat, discrimination, feeling undermined, unappreciated and bypassed. If we feel unable to reach out after loss, if we feel our grief to be too much for others, that we must bear it alone, our heart on all levels can feel more and more burdened, and our grief hardens down unmet.

> *The heart has its reasons, reason knows nothing of.*
> Blaise Pascal

If the heart is seen as 'nothing but a pump' and the feeling heart gets devalued, we are deprived of being able to listen to the communication of its symbolic language and its homeostatic function. For it is the energy and imagination experienced through our communication with the feeling heart that helps us to be in touch with our grief in a creative and useful way. We can then remain open to languages of communication and connection, listen and note the felt sense of our body, breathing and feelings.

As I have already mentioned I have a personal interest in studying the many different approaches to the imagination and function of the heart. In 1977 I was about to begin my psychological training when my late husband John McCormick had a serious heart attack while we were on holiday and was hospitalized for a month. We had been living together for just four months. This event, so early on in our relationship was a sudden brush with death. It invited us into the complex and mysterious world of the heart – the biological heart and the heart of feeling, of spirit. Away from home I was invited to stay with the family of the nurse looking after John. Her father was a Lutheran pastor. They had been through a great many difficulties in their lives and knew about suffering. They had learned to inhabit a real sense of collective presence, and a kind friendliness and stillness. This invitation to stillness and simply being with whatever I was feeling with acceptance and care was the first of many experiences I was to have and the beginning of my interest in the power of simple presence.

Their generosity to both of us was the first of many experiences we were to have on our shared journey with the heart and our understanding of the different qualities of the heart. We were brought into the very present fact of impermanence – a basic Buddhist description of how things are. Everything changes. We had a brush with death and were awakened into a new phase of life where the language of the heart was dominant, the reality of death was a close companion and being present with what we had in each moment paramount.

On our return home John asked his GP 'What do I do now?' and his GP answered, 'Just go home and relax'. It sounded simple, but how did he actually do this? He was a fit, lean man running a successful company and daring a new relationship. It was a huge shock, as it is for everyone, and he had to change his life and habits. We walked the streets of London around where we lived in the evenings to help relieve him of his frustration. He was angry about having a heart attack and beneath the anger was fear.

In a 1991 film by Mark Kidel made for Channel 4 called *The Heart Has its Reasons,* John described himself as feeling 'like a wounded animal in the jungle of commerce ready to be picked off by hungry competitors.'[23] This was a stark comment on what he later described as his 'super achieving assignment, working all hours, out until all hours, as if I was superhuman'. As the years went by the constant reminder of having to take continual care of and listen to his heart grew at the same time as our shared gratitude for life. He survived twenty-two years and died at Papworth hospital in 1999 after heart surgery. In those years we had the opportunity to have conversations we might otherwise have postponed and never stopped marvelling at being together and the miracle that was life.

My interest in the different studies and approaches to the heart both as central pump and as image grew. I became interested in how different people managed living with their heart when it had spoken dramatically as in a sudden heart attack. In 1984 I wrote a self-help book called *The Heart Attack Recovery Book* as I was interested in how families respond and cope with problems of the heart and its centrality to life, a powerful reminder of mortality.[24] How might families be helped with their fears of further loss, and not walk around on tiptoe in case of further attacks, holding their breath thus compromising their own hearts.

That same year, 1984, I was invited to work as a therapist in the Cardiac Department at Charing Cross hospital as part of cardiologist Dr Peter Nixon's team and began to learn much more about the heart. Peter Nixon taught that the heart is for effort – and that effort was multi-dimensional. This was at the time new to me and many others and certainly opened and widened our thinking and understanding. Every time we breathe, think, feel, move our body, the heart moves. It is the second strongest muscle in the body after the tongue. The heart can be taken out, cut, stitched and mended. When fresh blood flows once again through repaired arteries a patient is given a new lease of life, immediately, their breathing improves, circulation is improved, and they feel 'young at heart'.

The heart and the lungs operate together and the way we breathe is crucial. When anxious, sad, fatigued, stressed we tend to breathe shallowly and if this becomes habitual, we risk hyperventilation. Hyperventilation is a risk factor for coronary spasm and ultimately artery narrowing. Finding ways to learn to be aware of our breathing and learn abdominal breathing becomes crucial. At Charing Cross hospital this was taught by occupational therapists and nurses while distinguished medical personal researched into the effects of hyperventilation upon the heart. Developing the habit of being with the inbreath and outbreath so consciously is a basic meditation instruction across all disciplines. Learning and practising being still with our breath relies upon our noticing and quietening our busy mind, not following thoughts or feelings but letting them pass, like clouds in the sky. As we do this, we are quietening not only our mind, but the pressures within our hearts.

Dr Peter Nixon described behaviours such as trying to do more and more in less and less time and, often, under great odds which severely compromised breathing and the heart's function as 'hurry sickness'. I was at a meeting where one of the cardiology doctors mentioned that the wife of a patient who had just been admitted for urgent heart surgery had said to her that since his mother had died her husband behaved 'as if he could run past death itself'.

> We shield our heart with an armour woven out of very old habits of pushing away pain and grasping at pleasure. When we begin to breathe in the pain instead of pushing it away, we begin to open our hearts to what is unworked.
>
> Pema Chödrön[25]

PRESENT WITH SUFFERING

The heart is a powerful communicator. When we are able to learn to stop and simply notice what our heart may be indicating, become aware of feeling and match words for feeling, we are beginning a new relationship with our whole being. When we do first allow a pause or gap and notice the space in our chest we can call the heart space, we may find that hurt, bewilderment and other painful suffering arises. The physical and feeling heart are powerful communicators and need times when we are able to stop and carefully 'Mind the Gap' which we explore in the next section.

It can often be hard to express what are often seen as negative feelings after bereavement, but it is vital. Anger, rage and hurt are natural human emotions, particularly after loss, as is the often repeated question, 'Why, why now?'. All these experiences need to be allowed to rise and fall, be expressed in whatever way offers release over and over again. In a *Grief Observed* C. S. Lewis wrote about his loss of his wife Joy and about his belief in God being challenged: 'How could God be so cruel, what kind of God was he?'[26] He also wrote that the one consolation was that 'there was now someone to rail at'.

Many years ago, I saw a patient presenting with severe angina and high blood pressure. She spoke in a flat voice, on automatic. She felt irritated and impatient being referred to a therapist and thought her symptoms were just to do with doing too much. We sat together for a few sessions while

Heart

I heard about her children, her organized life packed with clubs and walking ... she rarely looked me in the eye and did not really want to engage. One day, as she took a big breath, I was able to notice and name this with her and, at first, she looked alarmed and waved at me. 'It's nothing,' she insisted, rubbing her chest. I asked if we might experiment together. She shrugged. I asked if she could put her hand on the area of the chest she had just touched to show me. She laughed harshly, looking really uncomfortable. 'It's nothing,' she said again, looking down.

But it seemed to me as if her hand had found itself on the area of her chest it had touched earlier and was acting as an unconscious messenger. Then I asked, 'What's it like?'

She shrugged. 'What do you mean?' her voice was haughty but there was a slight catch in it.

I smiled, 'If you could imagine it, a colour shape, image ...'

There was a short pause and then, almost despite herself she said, 'It's a red vase,' looking very surprised.

I passed her some pencils and paper and asked her to show me. I hoped that the illustration of what she had been telling me in words and what her body was expressing would be shared. She drew the red vase slowly, hesitated as she raised her head to look over the drawing and then drew a crack right down the middle with drops of liquid spilling out. When she looked up there were tears in her eyes. 'It's a red vase, a red cracked vase.'

It was a profound and powerful moment. Her emotion and feelings were strong. Then she said clearly: 'My heart is like a red cracked vase.'

We sat. I waited and was about to ask, 'What does this mean to you?' when she said, without hesitation, 'It's my divorce.' She wept quietly still clutching her chest.

This was the first time in the four years since her divorce that she had dared to express feeling. We were then able to enter into the process of grieving for her lost marriage consciously and together, writing letters she would never send, more drawings, releasing what had been held by her body but, I think, the most important fact was that this red cracked vase had come in with that moment of inbreath – and it was her own image, her own poetic imaginative resource. This process illustrates what can happen when we bring focus to the body and what it is holding and also when we allow the gaps to offer us their gifts.

Somatic Movement therapist Linda Hartley offers us a beautiful practice for an inner support for our hearts.[27] In this extract from a longer exploration, after connecting through the surrounding tissue layers to the heart itself, she invites us to:

- Sense-feel its three-dimensional, almost spherical shape, especially feeling into the back and underneath surfaces. Imagine the breath fills your heart, enters all the cells, nourishing and energizing them. Allow your heart to respond with a sigh, or a hum, or a note on the exhalation. Do you notice any sensations, or changes in your breathing? Does the presence of your heart feel clearer?
- Does your heart have a message for you? Listen with full and receptive attention. Enquire how your heart feels, what it might need to express or receive. Take as much time as you want and need here.

Loss and bereavement require effort of the body itself, muscles, nervous system, appetite and the heart in particular. As we learn throughout our experience to truly listen to the many different communications from our worker and feeling hearts we are entering new territory within which we may learn.

THE HEART AND COURAGE

However much our biological need for attachment has been successful and grown into giving and receiving love, all emotional intimacy demands courage. And this starts with ourselves, for we need to find the courage to become as close to our own emotional experience as possible, and the courage to accept and embrace it without judgement. In daring to risk opening to love in all forms, we risk loss.

In a play by Brian Clark called *Can you hear me at the back?*, the headmaster addresses the morning assembly after suffering a great personal loss and says he wants to talk about courage:

> The word courage comes ultimately from Latin through old French into English and it comes from the word coeur, heart. It was thought that the seat of bravery was the heart, which was also the seat of love. ... and that is no accidental conjunction, because to love is to be brave. It is to be open and defenceless even to that which would hurt us ... [And later:] when we have to accept, in love, a great blow, it requires the greatest bravery to continue to be open, receptive and not close up ...[28]

These are interesting derivations, that love, courage and heart are all connected.

But remaining openhearted is not easy. Simply living a life means that our heart space can feel bruised, dented, challenged and even attacked. Over and over again we are invited to notice that which can so hurt us, and find love for these parts of ourselves, and to others outside of us who are difficult to love. Our worker and feeling hearts have to find release and regain homeostasis, equilibrium, balance, and dare to become open to love again. Once more, Thich Nhat Hanh is my inspiration. In his poem *Call Me by My True Names* are these lines:

> The rhythm of my heart is the birth and death of all that is alive.
> Please call me by my true names, so I can wake up and the door of my heart could be left open, the door of compassion.[29]

We need a practice that helps our heart enter the lion's den of emotion not in a heart sink, sacrificial way, or in a heroic, conquering way. But as a vehicle that is actually quite simple, and modest, reminding us that the heart is the second strongest muscle in the body and also extremely sensitive, with its own intrinsic brain. We need to really understand what is meant by wellness, to keep well and do the things that maintain this wellness.

MINDFULNESS, *MAITRI* AND COMPASSION

As we saw in the first section, mindfulness offers us a way to remain with what is happening in the present moment, without judgement, without trying to change it or be overwhelmed by it. In *Breath by Breath* Larry Rosenberg writes:

> There is a basic mystery to this energy of mindfulness. It has no colour, no weight. You can't grab hold of it. But it is extremely powerful all on its own. When you direct it at a painful or unpleasant feeling there is a transformation. It is like the ancient idea of alchemy which was said to transform base metal into gold. The base metal is our craving, aversion or confusion. The fire is our attention. The hermetically sealed container is concentration. The gold that comes out of it is liberation. Sometimes the painful or unpleasant feelings become neutral or pleasant although that isn't the point. We're not trying to change anything. Mindfulness itself is a subtle energy with transformative power.[30]

Maitri, a Sanskrit word, may be translated as either unconditional friendliness or loving kindness. When we try to practise mindfulness, we may at first find it difficult! For we come up against our own preoccupations and judgements, our own demanding self. When we learn to practise in a spirit of *maitri* we can remember to be kind to ourselves, however often we may find ourselves in judgement or distraction.

Heart

COMPASSION

When I first began speaking about compassion practice in my psychological work, and the need for this to be nourished within ourselves first before it can be offered to others, many people were concerned about the practice sounding selfish. Breathing in and out of our own recognized suffering while in an embrace of loving kindness is to offer compassion – *karuna* – for ourselves, softening into our own pain. Thich Nhat Hanh recommends we greet our own suffering with these words: 'Hello my friend (fear, pain, loss, anger), I know that you are there, and I am here for you.' Sometimes we may touch this place with our inbreath and extend spaciousness around it, then on the outbreath breathe out any tension, or tightness.

In her book *Compassion* Christina Feldman writes that compassion is the most precious of all gifts.[31] It is the force of empathy in our own heart that allows us to touch the broken heart of another. True compassion begins when we notice the suffering in another and are touched and moved by it. True compassion invites us to become vulnerable, to share equally in another's pain and to send loving kindness and compassion from that place of opening within ourselves. We cannot offer true compassion for others without nourishing our own well of self-compassion. We can learn to offer compassion to

PRESENT WITH SUFFERING

others when our own heart is touched by another's suffering. We simply breathe in spaciousness and wish the other person well, sending them loving kindness and compassion. The full practice of compassion invites us to open our heart, first to ourselves, then someone we love, then those we don't know, then someone with whom there is conflict and finally all sentient beings including ourselves.

In his book *The Mindful Path to Self Compassion* Christopher Germer offers us this very powerful meditation on compassion:

Soften, allow and love.

Start by finding a comfortable position, close your eyes, take three relaxing breaths.

Bring awareness to your body and the sensations occurring there in the present moment. Find your breath in the heart region and begin to track each breath with mindful awareness.

After a few minutes, release your attention to your breath and let your attention be drawn to the place in your body where your difficult emotion can be felt most strongly.

Heart

Soften into that location in your body. Let the muscles be soft without a requirement that they be soft, like applying heat to a sore muscle. You can say 'soft … soft … soft' quietly to yourself to enhance the process.

Allow the discomfort to be there. Abandon the wish for the feeling to disappear. Let the discomfort come and go as it pleases, like a guest in your own home. You can repeat 'allow … allow … allow'.

Now bring some love to yourself for suffering this way. Put your hand over your heart and breathe. You can also direct love to the part of the body that is under stress. It may help to think of your body as if it were the body of a beloved child. You can repeat 'love … love … love'.

'Soften, allow and love.' 'Soften, allow and love.' Use these three words like a mantra, reminding yourself to incline with tenderness toward your suffering.

If you experience too much discomfort with an emotion, stay with your breath until it eases.

Slowly open your eyes when ready.[32]

Dr Germer's meditations are also available free of charge on his website: https://chrisgermer.com/meditations.

Mind the gap

> *One of the most effective things we can do when we see the gathering storm of our habitual tendencies is the practice of pausing or creating a gap. We stop and take three conscious breaths, and the world has a chance to open up to us in that gap. We allow space into our state of mind. Meditation practice itself is a way to create gaps.*
> Pema Chödrön, 2021, Lion's Roar Foundation

Emotional emptiness in relation to loss and bereavement is often associated with a gap that is painful and unwanted both internally and externally. It is a gap that initially we long to fill, to put the clock back in time to when our life with a loved one felt fresh, alive and warm. This section looks at how what has been experienced as a gap can be eventually transformed into a series of simple pauses or mindful spaces. Within these spaces we are able to develop the capacity to be present with our suffering, just as it is, without judgement. It's a gap or space that can include all our feelings, our sorrow, lament, our regret and our emotional pain without our being limited or overwhelmed by them. Where we can have moments of spaciousness around the density of our feelings and responses. It is by creating gaps in the busyness of our everyday minds that we develop the practice of mindfulness. Within this practice there can be the potential for moments of real peace, for loving kindness and compassion towards ourselves and our experience and also towards others. It is in the gaps we allow safely during these challenging times that we make a new living relationship with ourselves and our experience.

Throughout this part of the book on being present with loss and bereavement, we have explored the kind of experiences and fears that can obstruct us in finding peace and stillness: our attachments, fears of impermanence; the exhaustion in our body leaving little or no space; and the continual suffering emotions of our broken heart. In order to create a helpful gap, we simply stop and pause, maybe for just three breaths at first. In the pause we sit, allow each breath to be slow, in and out, we notice our body and any tensions it is carrying, and we release them. As we sit, we simply notice what arises in thoughts, feelings and sensations and we let them pass like clouds in the sky. We do this with softness and kindness towards ourselves. Using a mantra or simple phrase such as 'breathing in, I know I am breathing in' can help create a containment at the beginning of practice. When we realize we are drifting away into thoughts or sensations we gently bring ourselves back to the present and continue with the slow rise and fall of the breath. This simple practice helps us create a mindful presence with all that is arising, kindly, without judgement. It builds our inner strength with suffering.

In loss and bereavement, we enter into completely new spaces inside ourselves. These experiences are often non-verbal, sometimes returning us to early memories, early feelings of helplessness and fear. But we can learn to 'mind the gap' safely through the structure of mindful practice, by noticing and caring for all those experiences that arise, and not be flooded by them. This can take the form of just sitting or walking and concentrating on three breaths, in and out. At first this basic practice may be seen as simply 'something to do'. It is useful that it is called a practice because practising helps us to develop a routine structure for simply being. We may find that as we continue with practice, we experience moments of real stillness. This can be like touching something completely new, something previously unknown but something we all have the capacity for – moments of stillness. A still space where we are no longer limited by our history or perceptions. This is the beginning of healing.

The process of minding the gap allows us to differentiate between those sensations and feelings we are aware of inhabiting our bodies, and the ideas we cluster around them in our thoughts. For example: 'I feel sick, I'm never going to enjoy myself again; the pain in my chest is so huge I fear I will have a heart attack.' When we can allow, safely, some space for simply noticing our experience, kindly, we can begin to stay with it. We are also entering a world peopled by others who have suffered loss. I found this thought extremely helpful as a practice in the early years after my own bereavement – that I was not alone but treading well-trodden steps throughout the world.

There is something else that can arise when we 'mind the gap'. At a talk given in Oxford in 1985, the archetypal psychologist and Jungian analyst James Hillman suggested that 'Something lives in me that is not of my own doing'. He was referring to the mysterious energy in all of us that is not driven by the conscious ego but something we are born with, already there. If we are too busy or preoccupied to stop and mind the gap, we never know what these moments might illustrate.

John Weir Perry's research in the 1950s illustrated that some patients suffering psychosis spontaneously drew mandalas, images of wholeness, when offered art therapy by therapists who held a spiritual or transpersonal attitude.[33] This research supports the view that we all have the capacity for wholeness whether or not it is eclipsed by illness, ignorance or busyness. If we are aware of this potential, it can be our companion during dark times whether the moments of wholeness within us appear or not. Whenever we sit with others who also share the belief that humans are capable of having a meaningful relationship with suffering, we allow the potential of the pause or gap to offer us glimpses of peace, and images of wholeness might arise. Glimpses of our being more than the sum of the parts. Therapists who have their own contemplative or mindfulness practice, whose therapeutic work is nourished by their own practice, are able to just sit in the embodied space with another, listening out for the tone of the wordless places, the gaps between the words and allow whatever arises to be present. Kind attention can melt what has become the frozen ice inside us.

The more reflective and contemplative psychotherapies teach the art of listening and not just to words. An illustration of this is from Marie Cardinale's reflections on her time in analysis in *The Words to Say It* when in one of her therapeutic sessions she just turns over or sighs and the analyst leans forward and says 'yes … yes …' welcoming whatever needs to arise.[34] There can be a precious space that evolves when two or more people sit together listening deeply to each other, allowing themselves to be just what psychologist Carl Rogers called a 'shaky person', and with what Buddhist nun and teacher Pema Chödrön referred to on a retreat I attended at the Shambhala Mountain Center as 'shaky tenderness'. I found this a profound and helpful phrase throughout my working years as a therapist. It is curious that mindfulness practice encourages us to rest our attention on the present moment, with no other intention: nowhere to go, nothing to do. It is not about achieving anything. And yet, if we allow ourselves to open our minds to the possibility of the life that might arise in the pause, we are offering ourselves the opportunity for something already in potential but yet unnoticed.

When we no longer feel overwhelmed by what feels like the emptiness of the gap, or when we are less pressured into filling it with activity or substances, we are ready to explore a different experience of the gap. It is inbetween our preoccupations of mind that we are able to notice the sensations in our body and to really give them safe space. As we do this, we may also allow words to arise that best describe what our body is carrying. When there is a real fit between sensation and word, we experience what Eugene Gendlin called a felt shift.[35] This is a subtle movement within us linking body and mind and the connection this invites.

In the gap we are most sensitive to what is around us all of the time, silence, birdsong and music, the words of the poets, the words of wise others. It is then possible to experience the gap as an opening, a spaciousness for what has been unknown. We are born with the potential for listening to all levels of language as well as to the spaces between words or notes, to language that has not yet been able to be made conscious and thought about. Christopher Bollas names this potential as the 'unthought known'.[36] Once we are able to encourage and acknowledge the gaps in our continual everyday busyness, we allow a fresh energy to arise. Within this gap we may find a word, sound, image or simple stillness that is new, and wonderful.

Sometimes we find a poet inside us that leads the way like Grace Andren whose daughter died aged five:

Grief
In times of tragedy
In times of sorrow
Lend your arms
For a place to burrow
Lend your ears
To listen and hear
Just be there
Be near[37]

When we are ready to allow a gap to arise in our everyday life, we find that we all have the capacity to create our own form of poetry or collage that can be a companion on our path of suffering – weaving words, sounds or fabrics, finding within us a healing capacity and creativity we did not lose. This is both nourishing and also a stepping stone to the path of more formal mindful meditation if chosen.

PRESENT WITH SUFFERING

The London Underground uses this expression 'mind the gap' in warnings about stepping out of the carriage onto the platform when there is a gap. As we mind the gap in this familiar and practical way we are already practising with our minds and bodies not to fall into danger. When we mind the gap in whatever form it arises, we are learning to be present, bringing our attention to each moment.

In his Ted Talk, called *Mind The Gap*, Dr Andy Harkin, psychiatrist, psychotherapist specializing in working with the traumatized body, begins by quoting from James Joyce, 'Mr Duffy lived a short distance from his body …'[38] This can apply to many of us particularly after the shock of loss when we really don't want to be in our body with its physical reminders of loss and all the difficult feelings that accompany us day and night, reminding us that the person we loved is no longer alive. But, as we have seen in earlier sections, it is the body through which we become conscious and aware, that leads the way to our developing capacity to be in the present moment. Just present with the simple process of breathing in and breathing out.

Dr Harkin speaks eloquently about ways in which we may dare to find and enter the gap, to learn to pause and give our attention to the rhythms of movement always alive inside us, our own fluidity. He says: 'Movement is what we are.' This celebrates impermanence and we learn that suffering can be taken in a series of waves, one at a time. Our rhythms of breathing in and breathing out can be like the rise and fall of each wave in the ocean, one wave, one breath at a time. When we are able to tune into our undivided body we return to a sense of fluidity and our sense of living inside a body becomes less restricted and chaotic. Wellness is experienced as a felt sense and it takes just 30 seconds or three breaths to create a pathway to wellness that is very different from the medical model. As we move to mind the gap created by our thoughts around suffering, we come home to ourselves.

A Plum Village breath poem

I have arrived,
I am home.
In the here,
In the now.
I am solid and I am free.
In the ultimate I dwell.

As we saw earlier, my Buddhist teacher Thich Nhat Hanh experienced such rage and helplessness at the deaths of so many of his countrymen and women and monks during the Vietnam War that he had to just walk with all his difficult feelings, anywhere, for miles, in all weathers, until he could be still. Until his body and emotions were still enough to create a gap. This was the time when poems arose, and his book of poems called *Call Me by My True Names* speaks of our need to bring stillness into our lives. For him, the words that came from the wordless places were about the interrelationship between all animate life and death, enemy and friend, powerful and powerless, and that all of us are in a process of continuation. From this time, he developed what for the Plum Village monastics continues to be an important practice, mindfulness of walking. Sometimes this practice is done with just one step, one breath, touching the earth with grace and awareness, aware of sounds, smells, the feel of the air on our bodies. Aware of being alive. And of being present, in the present moment.

When he spoke at a retreat in Arnhem, the Netherlands – a place of great historical losses – he spoke about borrowing mindful energy from others when our own practice of mindfulness feels thin on the ground. This has been a novel idea within our own Sangha here in Suffolk where I live and found to be very useful. As we saw in an earlier section (page 51), when we practise offering compassion, we begin with offering loving kindness and compassion first to ourselves, and then to others, but when our own well is nearly empty, and we feel we have nothing to share we can draw on the energy of loving kindness all around us until our own well is replenished. When our own well of loving kindness and compassion is replenished, we are then able to give back the energy we have borrowed.

One last story comes from my own experience which I would like to honour for it altered my attitude to my own bereavement and to working as a therapist with loss and bereavement. It illustrates what can become possible when we mind the gap.

Twenty-two years ago, I felt all the feelings I have named here in this section, the sense of hopelessness, colourlessness; loneliness, darkness, the aching loss which is physical, feeling sick. Not sleeping or wanting to eat. Everything felt pointless. I felt that I would never feel happy again. My feelings were a mixture of numb and bland and, to an extent, I was on automatic. Every now and then an act of kindness would bring tears, connecting me with feeling, letting me know that I was still alive as a sentient being – such as when kind friends left messages on my telephone after I had been working away from home so that I did not enter a silent empty house; someone would send a poem, or bring flowers; friends and family would come to help me sort stuff out or deal with all the paperwork. There was then, and possibly still is, a profound sense of embarrassment for some about speaking to the bereaved, not knowing what to say, and loneliness would be magnified. As kindness began to make appearances everywhere and I began to receive these moments, I became aware of the power of the two-way experience of giving and receiving.

One day when I sat down to practise mindfulness of breathing, I looked at the carved wooden Buddha I had brought back from Vietnam. As I was breathing out and pausing at the end of the inbreath I had a sense of all the other people who had trodden on this path of bereavement, in whose footsteps I was following. It was as if they were beaming goodwill toward me. That the experience of bereavement was a rising and falling, like the breath, of emotion, thoughts, actions and that human beings can be in connection with all living things, the earth, sky, nature, and every person or creature that has gone on life's path before us. For me, what had felt empty was now experienced as a sense of myself in connection with all life, a process of continuation.

It was from my experiences of the slowly emerging gaps in the frozen ice of bereavement that I began experiencing what we could call moments of grace. Where I felt connected to more than just my own limited experience. I had had to move to a new house after six months and had made no bond with the place, experiencing it as cold and alien as I was. Until one day, after about two years, I opened the back gate and it was as if the house was smiling, as if it was saying 'Ah there you are at last'. I stopped astonished and then realized I too was grateful that the realization of 'Ah, there you are, thank you' was my own inner voice, my own reality and that yes, I was alive. In one of Plum Village meditations, we say 'present moment, wonderful moment'. This was such a moment. I really felt and allowed the connection and kindness to make all the difference. I began to be fully aware that I was not alone but walking in the footsteps of all the many other people who had lost loved ones. There is a well-trodden path.

We have seen that mindfulness meditation invites us to practise with *maitri* – unconditional friendliness. What arises in all of us when we allow a space can offer us such solace and beauty, such hope. In celebrating these moments we do not need to use words such as 'moving on' or 'getting over it' but allow for an inclusivity of both death and life. We can learn to track what we are feeling, somatically, and keep a journal of our feelings and experiences to reflect on, we can practise from breath poems, lines of poetry or lines from songs, or from exchanges with others. When we can begin to bring self-compassion into our meditation and practise this regularly, the practice can help us find healing and peace. Our suffering over our loss does not go away, but we now have several ways to practise being present with our suffering, kindly. All these rituals can help us out of the darker recesses of the cave as we lament what has passed and celebrate what is present.

PRESENT WITH SUFFERING

BE FREE WHERE YOU ARE

Thich Nhat Hanh remained in France for over forty years, welcoming people from all cultures and diversity, and the continuation of his work is celebrated all over the world. When he was invited to speak at the Baltimore Penitentiary, he invited the prisoners, many of them 'lifers', to 'be free where you are'. Even when imprisoned literally, metaphorically, or exiled from our country as was this revered teacher, we can choose to be free within ourselves, even if for just a few moments, and there are ways to learn how to develop this. After this talk, The Still Water Mindfulness Practice Community was established at the prison in 2015 and has been of huge help to the inmates.[39]

THIS MOMENT, THIS ONLY,
ALL THAT THERE IS

The 'mantra', *This Moment, This Only* came from a lay person's retreat given by a senior monastic at Amaravati Buddhist Monastery circa 2007. When our Sangha share this next meditation together I always know if I have been stressed or overdoing it as at first I find the pause very hard to find. There seems no gap … but it can arise from practice!

Mind the gap

Sit comfortably and allow any busyness of mind to settle.

Sit upright but not rigid.

Place your attention on the inbreath giving full freedom to the flow of air that slips down through the nostrils toward the throat, then the bronchi, and finally to the bottom of the lungs, before reversing its route on the inbreath.

Focus attention on each inbreath, and the gap at the top of the inbreath.

Follow the outbreath, the long exhalation of air as it leaves the body slowly, gracefully, all the way to the end, until there is barely a perceptible breath left.

Sink into the calm and peacefulness of the pause, just before the next inbreath which fills our lungs effortlessly, our breath like a wave, rising and falling.

This moment, this only, all that there is.

2

Emptiness

Nigel Wellings

First Thoughts

Form is emptiness, emptiness is form
The Heart Sutra

This is a piece of writing that started life as a talk. Not quite sure where to begin (and we will see how starting and finishing is a big deal when it comes to emptiness), I took from a selection of beginnings that give a taste of what will follow – here they are:

Although we think of emptiness as a painful psychological state, perhaps something to see a psychotherapist about or even take a pill, in Buddhism it is the ultimate truth, and the goal of all Buddhist meditations.

Pinning this talk on the word 'emptiness' is a little misleading. Within our own psychotherapeutic understanding, emptiness as an emotional state is synonymous with experiences of depression, meaninglessness, a sense of being without joy or direction, an absence of energy or libido. However, in the Buddhist context 'emptiness' is the English word of choice to translate the Sanskrit word 'shunyata' – an enormously rich and complex notion that has been unfolding in meaning for almost two-and-a-half thousand years. A notion that is the opposite of our own usage – for to directly and fully experience emptiness is the experience of unbounded bliss.

In fact, the Sanskrit word that most closely captures our understanding of emptiness is not 'shunyata' but the word 'duhkha' – a term that encompasses a spectrum of physical and mental pain from acute suffering to a feeling of pervasive dissatisfaction and discontent.

I have heard it said a number of times that Buddhism is the religion of choice for psychotherapists because it has such a sophisticated psychological understanding of why people suffer and what can be done about it. However, at the very heart of Buddhism is the notion of emptiness – the ultimate nature of things being entirely transitory and insubstantial – and in this it seems to contradict the psychotherapeutic goal of establishing a healthy sense of self that includes a feeling of substantiality and duration. From the Buddhist perspective on emptiness such a substantial and lasting self does not truly exist and, furthermore, the belief that it does is seen as the cause of endless suffering.

In Buddhism 'emptiness' is the Holy Grail. The direct, unmediated experience of emptiness is synonymous with complete spiritual awakening. To know emptiness entirely is to lose the self in rapture!

A meditation on the pain of emptiness

Pain is a given, but with suffering there are options.

Our lives seem shot through with many small unhappinesses, frustrations and occasionally something that really hurts. It does not seem to matter what we do, however many courses, self-help books or therapies, this pervasive experience of discontent and occasionally something worse will not go away. One of the ways our culture has responded to this is by finding value in suffering. The Analytical Psychologist C. G. Jung, deeply influenced by Romanticism, said that if we did not experience suffering we would be unable to experience its opposite. To value comfort and ease, companionship and love we need to know their absence. However, when I hear this, it seems a cold comfort. It may make for good poetry but most unhappiness has something about it that grinds us down; far from being ennobled we are diminished by it, worn out, emptied. This grimmer reality seems confirmed by how we are with the things that wound us. Rather than celebrating, we want everyone to know just how much it hurts as we reach out or feel shame as we hide ourselves away. I wonder as I write this whether these reactions go back into our mammalian past, an animal that crawls behind a rock or into a bush when wounded or having confidence in the benevolence of the pack or herd cries out for the safety of their numbers?

The Buddha, a student of being human and definitely not a Romantic, observed that while many things in his life were enjoyable and brought pleasure – he had after all known a privileged background, been married to someone he loved and had had a child – there was something still not right. The word he used to describe this 'not rightness' was the rich and complicated term *duhkha*. This is frequently translated as 'suffering' and is often extended to the dramatically morbid, 'all life is suffering'. However, this is not entirely correct. *Duhkha* also encompasses experiences that we would normally see as desirable. Some scholars, speculating on its meaning, believe that it originally described an ill-fitting axle in the wheel of a cart that caused a 'bumpy ride'. This seems to work better – life is a bumpy ride even at best. The Buddha, observing his bumpy ride, the unsatisfactory nature of experience even when things seemed to be going well, described three areas of discomfort. The first, the *duhkha of suffering*, was the most obvious. Human life is vulnerable and we often find ourselves experiencing physical or psychological pain. The second, the *duhkha of change*, similarly obvious, refers to the

A meditation on the pain of emptiness

inevitable loss of something we want and value – a person, a situation, our sense of who we are. The last, the *duhkha of conditioned existence*, is more nuanced. The Buddha realized that, however enjoyable, pleasures were short-lived and could easily become felt as empty. He had observed something we all know. A pleasure that ends before we want it to is a disappointment whereas one that goes on too long may become a burden or even repellant. Pleasure and pain are entirely dependent upon factors beyond our control and in themselves are not stable emotional states. *Duhkha* then encompasses a spectrum of experiences running from agony to boredom. Often described as pervasive 'unsatisfactoriness' we could also see it as a spectrum joined by the thread of emptiness, whether it be the emptiness of being worn down by chronic pain or the lesser emptiness of not knowing how to enjoyably spend a couple of hours during a rainy afternoon.

What follows is a meditation on suffering – not just a list of symptoms and their causes. Here meditation means reading it slowly if you can. Letting the reality behind the words penetrate. When I first read this to an audience there was a distinctive weight that settled on us all. Recognizing pervasive dissatisfaction, our discontent, is something that is usually avoided when possible and yet, as we shall see, this recognition is the essential first step.

EMPTINESS IS NORMAL

Given the pervasive nature of emptiness it is inevitable that we will all experience feelings of emptiness sometimes. However, when this becomes profound and chronic, it may be the cause for us to seek the help of a psychotherapist or counsellor. This is what several people I have spoken with have said:

> *It's like when you go out and buy a pair of expensive shoes you can't afford because you feel like rubbish inside. It lasts five minutes, it doesn't make you feel better. And then you look at your bank account and you feel even worse.*
>
> *I just don't feel anything. It's as if my emotions are flattened, there's just nothing there. I look in the mirror into my own eyes and they are dead.*
>
> *I am left feeling the emptiness inside, a great black hole of despair.*

FEELING EMPTY

Emptiness is what we feel when there is something missing inside. This could be because of a loss of someone or something important external to ourselves or it could be the loss of something important internally – perhaps a satisfying life that has direction and meaning. Essentially emptiness is an experience of being without, of not having – not having material belongings, not having answers, not having love, power or hope. Words that are often used as synonyms are being in a vacuum, being lost, being in a wasteland, a desert, adrift and all at sea.

CIRCUMSTANCES TRIGGER THE EXPERIENCE OF EMPTINESS

Where do we start, given there are so many circumstances that may include, alongside other emotions, feelings of emptiness: death, divorce, depression, terminations, illness, bankruptcy, failure, addiction, loneliness, isolation, identity confusion, loss of community, loss of belief, loss of a stage of life, fear of old age and death? Pervasive yet unidentified feelings of inner discontent, yet oddly also success, achievement and conquests (here think of empty or pyrrhic victories). And on a larger scale: powerlessness in the face of events, frustration with political madness, injustice, racial persecution and genocide, war, poverty, disease, degradation of our environment, loss of animal and plant species and climate change – the real possibility that we will destroy ourselves. And within society, with its depersonalization: the tendency for everything to be reduced to economics with us playing a meaningless part in the continuance of a consumer treadwheel, being the victims of faceless bureaucracies, faceless multi-nationals and faceless decision makers.

THE EXPERIENCE OF EMPTINESS IS PHYSICAL

Emptiness may be felt in the throat, the chest, the stomach, the genitals. It aches, gnaws, eats away, leaves us breathless, winded, choked and sickened. Like melancholia or depression, it weighs down upon us, it is heavy, leaden, immovable. We speak of the weight of grief. Without joy our libido is absent, closed down, relationship is an alien land. We are physically turned off, avoidant, not present. We are often left without words, speechless, mute. We can feel on the edge of tears but no relieving tears come. Or we can cry oceans and yet not really know where the tears come from nor why we weep. Full of emotions there is no transformative expression or catharsis. We are just stuck.

EMOTIONS ASSOCIATED WITH EMPTINESS

Emotionally numb, despondent, isolated and anxious. Bleak and barren, inhabiting a wasteland. Disconnected, disinterested and disengaged. Disinclined to enter into anything.

A meditation on the pain of emptiness

Without curiosity. Driven to fill the void, we engage in activities that are ultimately unfulfilling such as compulsive shopping, eating, sex or substance abuse – though it is we who are actually abused. Consumer culture capitalizes on feelings of emptiness, first generating them and then promising fulfilment with this or that product. But ultimately this may lead to feelings of being used or predated upon, furthering the feeling of emptiness.

And another twist, all these emotions may be a means to not feel other emotions that are felt to be threatening to our sense of self. Emptiness here is more like a void in which we avoid feeling what we cannot bear to feel. Emptiness then becomes a defence and, as a defence, we resist anything that might dismantle it, so in this sense emptiness is the preferred devil we know. It feels bad but it hides feelings that are even worse.

THE EXPERIENCE OF EMPTINESS IN CHARACTER STYLES

When developmental psychology and psychopathology are married we get complex systems that map how stages of maturation, when arrested by different degrees of hurt, express themselves in broadly recognizable ways. In each of these presentations, emptiness is felt differently. Here is one system based upon Stephen Johnson's *Character Styles*.⁴⁰ I have divided it into three periods: birth and infancy, establishing a separate sense of self and making relationships:

The schizoid wound – when we feel hated

As an intrauterine and just newly-born infant, when we sense a threatening physical/emotional environment and fear that we will be annihilated, we experience our universe as a malignant empty space and our own emotions as dangerous.

The oral wound – when we feel abandoned

Close on the heels of this, as an infant who fails to make a good attachment, not feeling the nourishment of our mothering person's love nor that our own love is received, we will experience this as the emptiness of physical and emotional hunger.

The symbiotic, narcissistic and masochistic wounds – when we feel used, owned or defeated

As a toddler making our way into the world we need to be allowed to go our own way a little, come to know ourselves through the reflection of others and not fear punishment when we get something wrong. When frustrated, these important developmental steps create experiences of emptiness that may be felt as an anxiety whenever we try to be separate or different, a fear of vulnerability and not knowing who we really are, and a subservience that hides a stubborn self-sabotaging will to survive.

The obsessive-compulsive and histrionic wounds – when we feel over-controlled or ignored or exploited

Finally, if, when we reach the stage of exploring all the relationships around us, we discover that the wild animal of attraction and desire within us is either repressed or is unseen or exploited by others, then the emptiness we experience here is either a controlling fear of our own sexuality and anger or a dramatic need to be seen and heard by others.

EMPTINESS AS A COMMON FEATURE WITHIN DEFINITIONS OF PSYCHOPATHOLOGY

- Depression: a sense of emptiness is related to feelings of hopelessness, loss of pleasure, low self-worth and low motivation. Sleeplessness and a loss of appetite – or the opposite, an unfulfillable gnawing hunger.
- Borderline personality disorder: chronic feelings of emptiness are associated with impulsivity, an unstable sense of self and suicidal fantasies/and self-harm.
- Alcohol and drug addiction: we may attempt to alleviate feelings of emptiness and depression by self-medicating.

The lack of availability of an addictive substance or attempts to quit using can also produce feelings of emptiness that are an aspect of craving. In fact to crave implies feeling empty.

- Schizoid personality disorder: a pervasive emotional detachment and absorption in our fantasies leads to an emptiness in our interpersonal life – an absence of close friends and the nourishment of emotional warmth.
- Schizotypal personality disorder: similar to above but here heightened by feelings of paranoia, thought disorder, feeling the world is unreal and having social anxiety. When we suffer this disorder we frequently behave oddly in conversation or in the company of others and become isolated. Here the pain of emptiness may not even be recognized.
- Post traumatic stress disorder – PTSD: experiencing disturbing thoughts and dreams, having uncontrollable flashbacks, being avoidant of any situation that may trigger the memories, our fight, flight or freeze responses are on continual high alert. Here the emptiness includes the isolation these experiences keep us in.
- Attention deficit hyperactivity disorder, ADHD: another wound where feelings of emptiness are not immediately known – so the difficulty of paying attention that in boys may manifest as restless activity and chaotic behaviour,

and in girls as a dreamy or inattentive absence. Here, as with other disorders, emptiness arises from the isolation and alienation that the disorder creates.

Emptiness is also associated with co-dependency, childhood emotional neglect and some forms of psychosis. It seems that emptiness is a common description for every sort of psychological malaise. To feel bad is often to feel empty inside.

EMPTINESS AS THE ABSENCE OF PLEASURE

The inability to take pleasure, anhedonia, is a particularly barren emptiness. To be surrounded by partners, family, friends and good circumstances and yet feel nothing of the happiness these sources normally brings us. This joyless place is associated with depression, substance abuse, psychosis and personality disorders. It cripples both wanting and liking, emotionally numb, without the feeling of pleasure that motivates us.

EMPTINESS IN THE EXPERIENCE OF SHAME

For many of us shame, self-criticism and self-recrimination are horribly present. This is particularly so when we feel some of the many manifestations of emptiness listed above. An inner voice tells us how bad we are, that there is something wrong, inadequate, pitiful and disgusting about us feeling like this. That other people are not like us, they do not indulge in such pathetic behaviours, they can achieve things we cannot. They are proper grown-ups while we are not. This corrosive way of thinking can come to haunt us and be deeply debilitating. Losing all confidence inside we cower away.

Buddhism calls these types of self-excoriating attack a 'second arrow'. (We will revisit this later in greater detail.) The first arrow that wounds us is the unavoidably painful emotions that just come with being a human being. This arrow we have no control over, life shoots us as and when it will. And yet, as if this is not enough, we then attack ourselves for feeling as we do, as if there is something reprehensible in feeling bad or sad, being angry with our fear, ashamed of our need. This self-inflicted suffering is the second arrow, but unlike the first that we can do nothing about, this one we can gradually learn to stop firing. One hurt is enough, why add a second?

EMPTINESS WITHIN THE THERAPEUTIC RELATIONSHIP

For those of us who work as analysts, psychotherapists and counsellors, when a patient or a client presents feelings of emptiness we may feel something of the same in ourselves when sitting with them. Perhaps our heart sinks at the thought of working with them, we may suddenly feel overwhelmed, not knowing what to say or do, we may feel deskilled, filled with dread or, perhaps more defensively, boredom or even anger. Words and ideas that we use to help us stay with these difficult emotions (or perhaps protect us against them) are counter transference, transference invitation, projective identification, co-transference and syntonic counter transference. However, this makes it all sound rather clinical and perhaps almost blaming. Quite simply humans naturally tune into each other and, if open, we feel something of what the other feels. When I feel empty you can feel empty alongside me.

SPIRITUAL EMPTINESS

Spiritual emptiness, for many of us, is initially unrecognized and presents itself in many of the forms we have considered above. Often originating in some form of emotional loss, the promise of the world fades and a longing for something else and more takes its place. There are many stories of saints and yogi's lives that start off with this kind of bereavement and then evolve into longing and the beginning of a spiritual quest. One such story is found in the accounts of the Buddha's life that started to appear around two hundred years after his death. Born into a local aristocratic family, his mother, Mahamaya, after dreaming she has been impregnated by a white elephant through the right side of her body, gives birth to a miraculous baby and then dies a week later. His father, Suddodhana, consults his astrologers to understand the meaning of these events. They say his son is destined to become either a great king or alternatively a wandering ascetic and renowned religious teacher. Unhappy with this, Suddodhana does his upmost to distract the Buddha-to-be – he is married at sixteen to the princess Yasodhara and at twenty-nine they have a son, Rahula. He is immersed in all the sensual pleasures that his lifestyle can buy. However, circumstances conspire, and during an unmonitored excursion through a local town his sheltered life is shattered when he witnesses old age, sickness and death and is appalled by the suffering that he now realizes he too will one day face. On his trip out he also sees a saffron-robed *samana*, we might say a spiritual dropout, and with this resolves to renounce his comfortable life for something that will never decay and to find refuge in something that can be entirely relied upon. This he calls *nirvana*, that which is 'unborn, unageing, undecaying, deathless, sorrowless, undefiled and utterly secure from bondage'.

A meditation on the delight of emptiness

I feel like I'm bobbing around in a sea of change.

At the heart of all Buddhist thought is the belief that once we know how things really are, once we see the underlying and continuously unfolding truth of things, we will be moved to live in a way that is both wise and compassionate. On a simple and immediate level, this means knowing what is happening within us – what emotions, thoughts and behaviours I am, in this present moment, experiencing. However, when we attempt to describe how things really are at the deepest level, the finally inexpressible mystery of emptiness, *shunyata*, different schools of Buddhist philosophy have each got something interesting to say.

NO ONE AT HOME – THE EMPTY SELF

After the Buddha left home he lived among others who like himself had renounced their previous life in the hope of finding something that would bring their suffering to an end forever. These groups held a variety of beliefs about our deepest nature. Some believed that each of us held within us a 'divine spark', a *jiva*, whereas others said that our self, *atman*, was identical with the underlying reality of the universe, *Brahman*. In contrast to these, the Buddha's final realization seems much less 'spiritual'. He said that when he investigated his own nature all he found was a complex process of interactions that made up the body and mind. Psycho-physical mechanisms that took the raw data of his senses and made meaning of it by drawing upon previous experiences. In Buddhist terminology the components of this process are curiously called the 'five heaps', *skandhas*, that make up the entirety of who we are. We are just sensations, feelings, thoughts, volitions and consciousness, and nothing more. No life spark, no true self at the centre. What is challenging for those of us who feel we do have a self, a real 'me' that remains constantly present except in deep sleep and perhaps coma, is that this insight contradicts this belief. Rather like contemporary neuroscience: while the brain simultaneously performs many functions that may be located in different areas, nowhere in this complexity is found a location that can be called specifically the site of the self. The activities of self-knowledge, self-reference and autobiographical memory may be located within specific areas of the brain but the self as a discrete entity in which these activities occur or are known has no particular place. Rather the self, the feeling of 'me', seems to be an epiphenomena, something that occurs as a result of all the parts working together rather than something in itself. This ephemeral self, seemingly impossible to locate or pin down, might also be called a dream or a mirage.

A meditation on the empty self

Here is a meditation that broadly follows the Buddha's enquiry. It is designed to lead us through an exploration of various areas of experience and concludes with looking for the self who is doing the exploring. Do not think of it as a 'mindfulness meditation'. To get the reward of doing this give it some time.

> Finding a comfortable seat that requires no effort to maintain, start by dropping all intentions to now 'do' a meditation. You are just sitting where you are. Very light touch. Curious.
>
> Resting in this relaxed way notice everything in your field of vision – do not stare or peer, look gently from the back of the eyes. If you drift off into thoughts just come back. No big deal.
>
> And the same for sounds, let the sounds come to you, do not reach out …

PRESENT WITH SUFFERING

And the sensations within your body …

Now notice the subtle categorization of what you are sensing. Some parts of your experience feel pleasant, some unpleasant and some neither. From our perspective, what they are is unimportant. It's just about noticing …

Now notice that there is another part of your mind, a more busy part, that is naming and categorizing the experiences you are having now. Is it wanting to have a certain type of meditation, not wanting something or simply zoning out, refusing to be present? This is not good or bad, just notice it.

Now notice whether all these thoughts are compelling you to do something. Just notice the feeling of the compulsion but do nothing …

Now notice how you know all this. All these sensations, judgements and desires to act are arising in consciousness in each moment. Notice how consciousness moves between focusing on one sense or another, the subtle feelings of pleasant and unpleasant, the wanting and not wanting, the

A meditation on the delight of emptiness

itch to do something. Notice how consciousness is continuously and effortlessly present. You do not need to create it, it is here already. Rest in this broader awareness and breath.

Finally try to identify or locate the 'me' who is meditating – not as an idea, but as something separate and unchanging from all those areas of experience you have been present with. Something separate that you can put your finger on and say that is me.

Having practised this meditation, it may not be immediately obvious that we cannot find an identifiable permanent self somewhere in the processes of perceiving, understanding and action. Leading others in group meditations similar to this and asking the question, 'Who is it meditating?' or 'When you look inside what do you find?', has often elicited unexpected answers such as, 'Something round and kind'. I suspect that we are all so deeply accustomed to thinking of ourselves as a 'me' who 'has' emotions and thoughts (a 'me' probably located in our head) that observing just the bare facts and not adding anything else is hard. And yet this is what this meditation seeks to reveal. Look beneath the surface and we will find this person we believe ourselves to be does not exist in the way we imagine. Although it is true that character traits, the individual personality, do seem to persist throughout long periods of our life, meditative investigation reveals that our sense of self, like everything else, is a continuous process of change. That there is no 'separate self entity' at the centre of my being that is permanent and is not completely dependent for its existence on the infinite web of interconnections that is the reality in which we all live. My closely guarded individuality, often troublesome, protected at all costs, turns out to be a tiny bit of everything else, all of which is in perpetual flux. This is the truth of how things really are. And this begs the question, if my self is indeed really like this, do I have the best relationship to it?

THE RIVER OF CHANGE

Today, as we enter climate change and witness the destruction of our environment and many of the species within it, we are not left in any doubt that the world and we who share it are one vast ecosystem that is entirely dependent on all its parts for its survival. The details of this, for instance illustrated by Isabella Tree's arresting book *Wilding*[41] and Peter Wohlleben's *The Hidden Life of Trees*[42], are nothing short of wonderful and are one of the very many ways that we are brought to recognize the astonishing intelligence and beauty of the web of our existence. However, although

A meditation on the delight of emptiness

we are generally aware of the interdependent nature of our world and ourselves, we perhaps continue to think of it as a kind of mechanism in which all the tiny cogs are connected and work together. That each part of nature and the whole of the universe is made up of elements that may be named and in their naming become recognized as separate things that exist in intricate relationships. In this section on emptiness we will see that this view – though kind of correct – does not go quite far enough.

The Heart Sutra

Over fourteen hundred years ago, the Heart Sutra was composed. Today its succinct beauty is chanted in Buddhist monasteries daily. Said to have been taught by the Buddha to a group of accomplished bodhisattvas, it offers the essence of a newly evolving vision that became known as Mahayana Buddhism – the Greater Vehicle to awakening. In it we overhear a conversation between the embodiment of compassion, the bodhisattva Avalokiteshvara, and Sariputra, the Buddha's principal student – it concerns a more profound understanding of emptiness.

The body, feelings, perceptions, volitions and consciousness, and other descriptions of what constitutes our body and mind, are all declared to be 'not separate self-entities'. This enigmatic and ecstatic assertion drills down into the

Buddha's understanding of the absence of a permanent and separate self and takes it deeper. Early Buddhism had taught, as we have seen above, that beneath the level of awareness the body/mind was nothing but a series of fleeting states – a continuous ever-changing flood of sensations, emotions and thoughts. These were named *dharmas*, physical and mental events that, rather like atoms, were considered the 'basic stuff' or fundamental building blocks that the illusionary self is made of. But this new vision took this much further. If emptiness describes the seamlessness of all things, that it is impossible when we really closely look to locate a boundary where one thing ends and another begins, then this idea about the *dharmas* as discrete entities – separate things – must be wrong. How things really are cannot be a long sequence of rapidly changing independent physical and mental states. Rather, the deeper truth is that reality is more like a river where all its elements are not divided and, having no beginning or end, is a flowing and indivisible expression of an ever-changing whole. Or another analogy – reality is all one cloth, it has no seams joining parts. With this insight the nature of who we really are evolved; the very notion of things beginning and ending was destroyed because there were no standalone 'things' in the first place. Reality becomes an unimaginable net of infinite connectivity, emptiness as a process of profound, radical change paradoxically reveals the impossibility of both birth and death. As the sutra says:

> Listen Sariputra,
> all phenomena bear the mark of Emptiness;
> their true nature is the nature of
> no Birth no Death,
> no Being no Non-being,
> no Defilement no Purity,
> no Increasing no Decreasing.[43]

The Middle Way

While the Heart Sutra articulated this mystery through poetry, some time around the second century CE, Nagarjuna, a philosopher monk from southern India, approached emptiness through logic. He asked how our perception is so clouded that in place of the delight enabled by knowing how things really are, we instead experience pervasive dissatisfaction. His answer to this question is called the Middle Way – the middle way between things either existing or not existing. Things do not exist in the way we normally perceive them – as separate entities that have a (relatively) permanent existence. However, they do exist as an expression of the web of interdependent change that is perpetually in flux. That is, how things really are, their true nature, is the nature of emptiness. This is not simply a philosophical point. Direct, experiential knowledge of the Middle Way has a profound effect upon the experience of our life. As Shunryu Suzuki Roshi says:

When you do not realize you are one with the river, or one with the universe you have fear. Whether it is separated into drops or not, water is water. Our life and death are the same thing. When we realize this fact we have no fear of death anymore, and we have no actual difficulty in our life.[44]

Conventional and ultimate truth

Nagarjuna believed that our misperception of how things really are, our failure to recognize emptiness, is caused by the way we 'freeze frame' segments within the continuous flow of experience and then give these separate 'bits' a name that turns them into standalone things. We make things concrete. This is true not only of the world around us but also of who we consider ourselves to be. Try checking this out; look around your room – can you find something you do not have a word for? Then do the same for yourself. Even something unknown is called 'unknown' or 'inexpressible'.

This creates a world of named things that is responsible for the delusion that things exist as separate self-entities. A chair is a chair, I am myself, everything distinct and separate from everything else. Nagarjuna called this way of perceiving

A meditation on the delight of emptiness

'conventional truth' – the way we normally experience things. On the one hand, this has distinct advantages. It is simply how human brains work and it has enabled us to interact with our environment and our own psyches in a way no other creature can match. Without this facility we would be unable to identify and write about emptiness. However, it has a big downside. Many of the things we identify become the focus of attachment and this creates unhappiness. Living in a transitory universe, things change and if we resist this then loss is inevitable.

However, when we perceive things as they really are, knowing their emptiness, *shunyata*, then we see the 'ultimate truth'. The world as an infinite web of changing, interdependent processes that the conventional perspective dissects into the illusion of separate parts. Here emptiness is not an underlying reality that the universe is created from but more simply shorthand to describe its transitory and contingent nature. This deepening of perception, from conventional to ultimate truth, is mirrored in contemporary quantum physics. Common sense says we live in a world made up of things that are solid and real. However, when this world is closely scrutinized, it reveals that at the subatomic level it consists of empty space, protons, neutrons and electrons. And deeper still, elementary particles such as quarks whose nature is relationship. As the Buddhist scholar Peter Harvey says, 'Matter turns out to be a mysterious field of interactions, with "particles" not being real separate entities, but provisional conceptual designations.'[45] Nagarjuna's view entirely.

Beyond words

Nagarjuna used logic to demonstrate the Middle Way. Taking physical and psychological things such as motion, the elements, suffering, the self and entities, he pushed the arguments for their existence to absurd ends, finally demonstrating that on the ultimate level it is impossible to say anything about anything. In this way he leads us to an experience of a finally ineffable universe where the ultimate truth of how things really are transcends logic, words and concepts. A place that can be directly known but not really spoken of. Anything we may think or say is not *it*. However, that does not mean there can be no *hint* of something beyond words. For this we have two strange words that translate *tathata*, 'suchness' or 'thusness'. I find these impossible to understand conceptually – although I will give a definition in a moment. Rather, they are the kind of thing we might suddenly grasp or get a feeling of, an intuition, a flash of insight. The suchness or thusness of things is their very just-as-they-are-ness prior to thinking about them and pinning them down in words. It is ultimate truth shining through the conventional revealing in ordinary things their real nature, the common denominator of their emptiness. A timeless quality the Perfection of Wisdom sutras speak of as *anutpada*, having no origin.

This interpenetration of the conventional and ultimate truth means that the world of suffering and liberation from it, *samsara* and *nirvana*, are not two separate realities but more simply emptiness experienced either through obscured or awakened perception. As such we ordinary beings are already buddhas; could we but know it, *nirvana* is already present. Spiritual awakening is not so much about changing ourselves to become more spiritual but rather uncovering or recognizing the emptiness already present. Sharon Salzberg, awed by her visit to the Holocaust Memorial Museum in Israel, speaks of this interpenetration:

> *When we look within ourselves, we discover*
> *all beings and all things in the universe. Every*
> *event, every entity, every mind-state, every*
> *experience we have, is born out of a web of*
> *interconnectedness … A vast multiplicity of*
> *causes come together, ceaselessly, to produce what*
> *we call ourselves, what we call life.*[46]

THE PRESENT PAST

Some time ago I watched a TV programme demonstrating how our brains create our reality. Participants fitted out with special glasses that tracked the movement of their eyes were shown a large and dramatic painting of a group of people in a room. The glasses then conveyed what they had actually looked at onto a computer and this made it possible to monitor exactly what they had seen and what not. Then a researcher asked each person about the painting – what was happening within it? Astonishingly there were enormous discrepancies between what they had looked at and what they *believed* they had seen. Whole narratives were constructed from just a few details. Basically much of it was simply made up.

This goes deeper still. At the centre of our brain is a small area, the shape of an almond, called the amygdala. It is part of the limbic system which is concerned primarily with emotions and it plays a central role in keeping us safe by identifying either threats or opportunities. I find myself explaining this a lot to the people I work with in psychotherapy because it is such a valuable piece of self-knowledge. I say it is as if we have within us a person on a lookout tower in the middle of a clearing. All day and night they are on watch and they are particularly attuned to danger. When something emerges from the trees surrounding the clearing they are immediately alert and to help them identify what it is they have a large set of drawers that contains, in the form of coloured pieces of glass, all their memories. From these drawers they quickly take a piece of glass that seems to roughly fit and then, looking through it,

A meditation on the delight of emptiness

they colour the present experience with memories of the past. Then, if believing a threat is approaching, they slam their hand down on a big red button that triggers fight, flight or freeze reactions and the adrenaline needed to fuel them. Although there are obvious benefits from doing this, the problem is this also entirely obscures seeing things in a fresh and open way. Furthermore we frequently see danger when there is none. We are reacting to the distortion of our own memories held deep within the body rather than seeing things as they really are.

I suspect this activity was observed by two north Indian Buddhist monks, the brothers Asanga and Vasubandhu. Sometime around the late fourth to mid fifth century CE, they laid the foundations for a new understanding of emptiness which became called 'The Yoga Practice School' or 'Mind Only'. Similarly concerned with what distorts our perception, their insights were derived directly from the practice of meditation. Two signature teachings come from their work: the first describes how deeply unconscious patterns colour the present and the second how this may be undone.

The storehouse consciousness

Buddhism has always struggled with the intellectual problem of how karmic patterns are transferred from one life to the next if there is no enduring self – what 'carries' them across?

A variety of answers has been tried and the idea of the storehouse consciousness has grown out of these. It goes that we have eight levels of consciousness: five are the consciousnesses of the senses, one is the mind acting as a central receiving and primary response station, one organizing what is sensed into subject and objects – me and what I experience. The deepest one is the storehouse consciousness that 'contains', or perhaps better 'is', the continuity of the deep habitual patterns created in the past that perpetuate the complexities of the present.

Psychotherapists have wondered whether the idea of a storehouse consciousness, the *alaya-vijnana*, might correspond to the idea of the personal unconscious or even the Jungian notion of a collective unconscious – the repository of the physical and psychological templates necessary for being human. However, I think it is clear that the storehouse consciousness cannot correspond to the collective unconscious because, though inter-generational, its contents are pre-personal. What offers a better parallel, if we are not too concerned about reincarnation, is the person on the watchtower who we met above and the set of drawers that contain the coloured glass of our memories, the amygdala and hippocampus. Both are implicated in the reception of sensory information which they then assess for threats. When working well, being neither stressed nor traumatized, they more or less correctly evaluate and categorize our experience, but, as the levels of stress and trauma increase, so do their levels of misperception. This is made particularly so when, for instance, difficult infantile and childhood memories are triggered or when we are suffering from PTSD.[47] This then warrants the need for caution – at the very least, my emotions may feel real but these feelings are not necessarily true.

Seeing clearly

Although the Yoga Practice School clearly describes in detail how our perception is distorted, what it has to say about emptiness is a little harder to grasp because its understanding evolves over time. However, this evolution is extremely important because it sets the scene for changing the meaning of the word emptiness as shorthand for the transitory and contingent nature of everything to a description of the ground of being that may be directly known.

When we explored the Middle Way above we discovered that conventional and ultimate reality indivisibly interpenetrate in the same way that ordinary and subatomic reality are not two different things. As the Heart Sutra puts it – form is emptiness and emptiness is form. This is paralleled in the Yoga Practice School by a description of two ways of seeing how things really are – one an illusion and one accurately – and how our perception is 'perfected' or 'consummate' once we can distinguish between them. Together, these three ways of perceiving are called somewhat misleadingly the 'three natures', suggesting a similarity, when in fact they are radically different. The illusionary way of perceiving is the same as conventional reality – a world made up of separate things that appear to exist and are real. The accurate or true way of perceiving is described slightly differently – remember this description comes from the observation of yogis practising meditation, not a philosopher. So how things really are is an endless and indivisible flow of experiences that are conditioned by past karma that is held in the storehouse consciousness. This is where it gets hard to talk about it. I can easily describe going for a walk with my dog in a wood and the sights and sounds I saw there. The path through the trees, the light on the leaves, sounds, smells, the fun of seeing my dog ecstatically sniffing. But once I let go of conceiving it as many separate things, each with a name, and try instead to know it as a seamless flow of experience that is not made up of parts, the 'thusness' we touched in on above, then words fail me. Try imagining experiencing yourself in the wood with the dog without words or concepts right now – it leaves the mind flailing about. Once again we are back with the ultimately ineffable nature of reality – a holy mystery!

Perhaps because of the impossibility of putting this real nature of things into words it engendered much speculation. Some wondered what would happen to the store of karma

A meditation on the delight of emptiness

once meditation had purified the mind and the karma was exhausted – would things look different, would there be 'pure vision'? Whilst others thought that this level of consciousness might just disappear altogether leaving a transcendent mind that was somehow free from containing any appearances. These lines of enquiry opened into the possibility that the flow of experience may be known in two ways, one through the illusionary way of seeing we have already described – a world of named things that appear to really exist. And one through the perfected nature that recognizes that the world of appearances is solely known in awareness (how else or where else could it be known?), and, furthermore, the appearances that are known are not separate from the awareness itself. Just pause and think about this, it can only be true. The world around me and what I call 'me' are only known in awareness and it is completely impossible to know anything beyond awareness. Or said slightly differently – I do not have awareness within me; more accurately 'I' arises *within* awareness. With this leap of insight, emptiness took on a whole new positive dimension which is fully explored in sutras concerning buddha-nature, the awakened mind.

PRESENT WITH SUFFERING

WHAT WE FIND BENEATH OUR BED

Sometime between Nagarjuna and the brothers Asanga and Vasubandhu the first buddha-nature sutra was written. Most of us when we come across the buddha-nature sigh in relief. The Buddhist addiction to saying nothing in the positive because of the fear of being misleading here is abandoned. As I have said elsewhere:

> The message of these sutras is both simple and beautiful. All sentient beings already have buddha-nature from beginningless time. Therefore the purpose of the path is to reveal it, not create it. Buddha-nature is not something that arises from causes and conditions, already perfectly existing, it is fully recognized by removing the ideas and emotions that obscure it. Metaphors that describe this are that it is like the sun temporarily obscured by clouds, like butter hidden within the milk, gold hidden in ore and it is a treasure hidden beneath a pauper's bed. It is a potentiality that is both the ground of being, the path that discovers it and the final realization of its presence. To not realize this is to continue in suffering, to recognize it is to awaken. In this context emptiness continues to mean that the ultimate truth of all phenomenal things is that they do

not truly exist as discrete unchanging entities but the ultimate truth of buddha-nature is that it is empty – without – of any stain of ignorance. As perfect wisdom, pristine awareness, uncreated, timeless, free from extremes, the unity of emptiness and clarity, buddha-nature exists entirely without blemish.[48]

This understanding of our innermost nature, in the later non-dual traditions of Buddhism, Dzogchen and Mahamudra in Tibet, and Chan and Zen in China and Japan, became of central importance. It radically revisioned the path. If the treasure is already beneath our bed we need not create anything; rather we are uncovering what is already here. This is the foundation for the 'doing nothing' meditations we will visit at the end of the book. Here our buddha-nature is equated with what the Dzogchen tradition describes as the 'nature of mind', a state of spacious awareness that is empty, clear and compassionate. An awareness that is likened to the infinitude of the wide-open, cloudless sky.

HOW EMPTINESS CHANGES

So emptiness itself has unsurprisingly been on a journey – it too has changed. We started with looking for a sense of self that really existed, here meaning permanent and not a cause of all sorts of suffering, and what we found was a complex interaction of physical and mental states that are perpetually in flux. The self turns out to be a flow that comes and goes. This was followed by the Middle Way that deepened this insight by saying, if everything is actually in perpetual change, how can there be beginnings and ends and with this stepped beyond birth and death, being and non-being. Here emptiness takes on a further meaning – it is the inexpressible interdependency and impermanence of everything in which what we call 'me' is a fleeting illusion: 'a dream-like self in a dream-like world'. This was followed by the Yoga Practice School which with a skip and a jump, a sleight of hand, flips emptiness into a new meaning. When we take away the distorted perceptions that obscure how things really are, we enter a world of pristine awareness that defies definition. A world that is empty of any delusions. And finally this brings us to the emptiness of the buddha-nature; now a wholly positive description, emptiness is no longer about negation or absence but gloriously about the presence of the awakened mind once the emotions and thoughts that covered it have been released. This story is about disclosure – nothing need be created because buddha-nature, synonymous with how things really are, the ground of being, pristine and pure non-dual awareness has never for one instant been absent. Turn over the stone and there it is.

Being present with emptiness

To realize pure mind in your delusion is practise. If you try to expel the delusion it will only persist more. Just say, "Oh, this is just delusion", and do not be bothered by it.

Shunryu Suzuki Roshi

As we have seen in the first part, life brings its challenges and problems. However, as we have also seen in the second part, when we look deeply into these painful experiences we find that nothing is quite as stuck or solid as it initially appears. We also see that what we are experiencing in the present is largely our past and – such a relief – there is an experience of wide-open spacious awareness, our awakened nature, that may provide a refuge from the exhaustion of ourselves. In this last part, we bring these two together although the truth is they have never been apart. The path to emptiness as liberation is working with emptiness as suffering. Learning to be mindfully present with the unwanted parts of ourselves, our troubled emotions, intrusive thoughts and destructive behaviours is the gateway to something different. Seen in this way, awareness is the bridge between emotional emptiness and the emptiness as our innermost nature.

Some years ago I was sitting outside a conference room waiting to listen to Jean Marc Mantel, a French psychiatrist and teacher of Advaita Vedanta – an ancient practice of non-dual awareness. Sitting next to me was a slightly odd little man who seemed to have a kind of radiance about him. Initially this was unsettling and then I realized it felt rather nice sitting there – I was picking up what he was feeling. Of course it turned out I was sitting next to Mantel himself. Much of what he said was remarkable and there was no doubt that he was talking from his experience and not just theory. One image remains. He said that our ordinary mind full of thoughts and the spacious awakened mind, what he called the 'background silence', are very close to each other. It is as if we normally exist with our face in a bowl of water or in a cloud but it only takes a very tiny backwards movement to come free.

The Buddhist approach to finding the background silence is taken in manageable steps. In this section these are first establishing a good relationship with ourselves through keeping good relations with the world. This includes a look at generosity, the Five Precepts and loving kindness and compassion. Next, we make choices about what we allow our minds to do – we need not always be carried away by thought. This is followed by methods to calm the mind and work with our emotions through our body using the 'felt sense'. And, finally, stepping back from identification with our story into awareness – a new relationship to ourselves where emptiness is known as an expanse of space and clarity.

HAPPY RELATIONS WITH THE WORLD

Abstain from evil,
cultivate what is good,
purify the mind,
this is the teaching of the Buddha.

Dhammapada, verse 183

Some years back I read on Facebook an entry by a Buddhist academic claiming that those of us who had learnt secular mindfulness from an internet application such as Mind Space or a Mindfulness-Based Cognitive Therapy course could not expect it to work unless our meditation rested on a foundation of ethics, *sila*. Was this true? The Buddhist explanation is entirely practical. A mind that is caught up in doing harm is going to be disturbed and this will make it impossible to settle. The path must begin with moral virtue and from this grows freedom from remorse which leads to gladness, joy, a calm mind, insight and finally liberation.

I think of ethics – a rather dry-sounding subject – as the way we choose to treat ourselves, each other and the world we share. As we have seen, we are not separate from each other; emptiness means that it is all about relationship. In Buddhism, this is understood in the context of two key ideas, karma and rebirth. We could say that through these the consequences of our actions, the way we relate, are played out. The word 'karma' means action – good and bad. To make a karmic imprint we must have an intention that leads to events that we are satisfied with. This need not be conscious; karma, though less strong, is also created when these factors are not all present or are performed unconsciously. Once we have created karma it will come to fruition in this or a future life. However, this is not fatalism. We always have choices and it is possible to prevent the fruition of bad karma by denying it the conditions needed for ripening through interventions such as understanding and taking responsibility for what we have done and trying not to allow it to happen again. Buddhism also believes that the impulse of actions goes on eternally. Causes cause further causes and in this way the cycle of birth, old age, sickness and death is repeated until it is interrupted and finally ended through the intervention of awareness. However, optimistically, each of these infinitude of lives – if born with the good karma of a human – offers the opportunity for enlightenment.

Although these ideas may remain alien to many of us they do contain some basic common sense. Although I remain agnostic on rebirth – wavering, depending on whether the future is a place I want to be or not – as a psychotherapist I am convinced by karma. My psychoanalytic training confirms this at every turn. Just within a single lifetime the circumstances of our birth, childhood and adolescence repeatedly play themselves out during our entire life unless we consciously intercede and attempt to do something different. It may not be as mechanical as the Buddhist view suggests but the key point, actions have consequences, stands. Knowing this, we cannot finally evade the need to take responsibility for ourselves. Buddhism frames this responsibility as making skilful choices that encourage what is wholesome. This has nothing to do with things being sinful or wrong, but much more practically recognizing that some things create well-being whereas others do not.

Rick Hanson, a psychologist who has written extensively on neuroplasticity and Buddhism says that we are literally creating our brain by what we do with our minds.[49] If we choose to encourage violent fantasies, nurse resentments, envy and hate, then these will create neural networks in our brain that will then encourage further experiences of these fear-driven emotions. But the opposite is also true. When we choose to be skilful, encouraging wholesome mind states such as loving kindness, compassion and the celebration of the happiness of others, then these too will create neural networks that further support these qualities. As Hanson says, 'Grow the good that lasts'. Instant karma in action.

What constitutes skilful and wholesome actions is found throughout Buddhism. These are described within the Noble Eightfold Path – Right View includes taking responsibility for ourselves, Right Thought encompasses turning ill will and cruelty towards unconditional friendliness and compassion. Right Action, speech and livelihood all concern how we care for each other and Right Effort is the monitoring of what we let go of or encourage within our mind. There are also the Five Precepts for the lay Buddhist – not commandments but something we aspire to keep while knowing we will frequently fail – to refrain from killing, stealing, lying, harming others sexually and becoming intoxicated. But these all begin with generosity.

Generosity

From a Buddhist perspective, generosity, giving, *dana*, is the foundation of the path. And yet there is something quite tricky in this seemingly selfless act. If I am giving to gain something for myself, is my gift actually an act of generosity? Pema Chödrön, a much-loved American Buddhist nun, tells a story about giving some money to a man begging outside a food store. As she walked away he called after her – she had given him a large denomination note, had she made a mistake, perhaps she should have it back? It is a good story because Buddhism recognizes the fact that when we give it does something good for us as well. In Buddhist terminology this is called 'merit' which is what is accrued through acts that create good karma. However, had Pema Chödrön given with the accumulation of merit in mind, the amount of merit she would have gained would have been much less than that gained by the beggar with his spontaneous open-hearted generosity. The message is clear, there is giving and truly selfless giving.

The act of giving provides a rich object of mindfulness. As someone brought up to be careful about money and possessions – my wife would say stingy – I sometimes find it difficult to be as generous as I would like to be. I tend to look at each situation and think about it rather than just giving without consideration, knowing that the act itself is valuable irrespective of the recipient. As a French saying goes – giving with an open hand. What I have observed in myself is that my ability to give is directly linked to my sense of inner richness, my feeling full, or the opposite, my sense of being impoverished. Furthermore, I can sense these two states, fullness and impoverishment, within my body as a felt sense. The first feels expansive, more transparent and the latter more contracted, dense and dark. It is strange, one day I will pass a beggar or open an email asking for support and something small in me refuses to let the other in. I have a closed, unhappy heart. And then on another occasion I am

PRESENT WITH SUFFERING

open, their situation is painfully real and not wanting them to suffer, I eagerly give.

In Buddhist countries in which the lay community support the nuns and monks, providing them with food, medicine, clothes and shelter, the mutual benefit of giving and receiving can be clearly seen. For the lay person, supporting the monastic community is considered a rich source of good karma, a way of gaining the merit that creates the conditions for their own awakening. And for the monastics, women and men, their gift of teaching the Dharma that leads to awakening is considered the greatest gift of all. These gestures of generosity are encouraged in many ways. One is the Jataka Tales that recount the activities of the Buddha during his previous lifetimes while he was still a bodhisattva on the path. One story, which I have a personal and uncomfortable association with, tells of him meeting a starving tigress who was struggling to feed her cubs. This scene is created in papier mâché at a sacred site in Nepal where it supposedly occurred. The Buddha stands with his arm outstretched, offering it to the tigress as food. She stands before him, mouth open and behind her in a line sits her hungry brood. Unfortunately, this much revered tableau has become damaged from the touch of hands reaching out to receive a blessing. Furthermore, those wanting a blessing tend to push from behind, so on the occasion I found myself immediately before this sacred icon,

I was over-balanced and reaching out to save myself was in serious danger of catching hold and breaking off the Buddha's already fragile arm. Luckily I did not, but I still wonder about the labyrinthine calculations concerning the merit such an act would have incurred should it had happened.

On a more serious note, the Buddha talks about generosity in the first extensive account of the practice of mindfulness, the *Satipatthana Sutta*. Here, in the section that describes the necessary qualities for awakening, he includes rapture and joy and says that these may be increased by the recollection of acts of generosity performed by oneself and by others. This returns us to our first question. If I give to benefit myself how valuable is that? Here the answer is that even a selfishly motivated gift has value because it nonetheless still benefits someone else. But certainly, rejoicing in open-hearted, purely motivated acts of giving – knowing the good that this will bring to others – is better still. In these instances it is not 'all about me' but, putting our own involvement to one side, we focus on the primary Buddhist concern of doing no harm and increasing the good. This is also emphasized by generosity being the first of the 'six perfections', *paramita*, that a prospective bodhisattva cultivates, the others being morality, patience, diligence, meditative concentration and wisdom. Again, generosity is the ground everything grows from; we are told it creates well-being, happiness, a harmonious appearance and most importantly the fearless openness that is necessary for spiritual transformation. In direct proportion to our generosity comes a reduction in our possessiveness and an increase in our sensitivity to the feelings and needs of others. Generosity is non-attachment and friendliness in action. It is an awakened quality that springs out of us once the fear that obscures knowing how things really are begins to recede. Generosity is the fruition of the path spontaneously expressing itself.

Five good things

Accompanying generosity are the Five Precepts. These a lay Buddhist aspires to observe – five unwholesome actions that we try to not do. The first of these is killing and it comes as a surprise that human beings are not as murderous as it may seem. Matthieu Ricard, a French scientist turned Buddhist monk, in his encyclopaedic book *Altruism* documents how unless a soldier is trained while still in their late teens – prior to the full development of that part of the brain that regulates emotions – their natural empathy and self-protection will cause them during a battle to shelter and not shoot their weapon.[50] Those who do kill are a tiny minority of psychopaths, 1 or 2 per cent, who do so with relish. Furthermore, research into the origins of our species suggests that for the first 98 per cent of our history organized conflicts between groups – war – did not exist and only began about 10,000 years ago when nomadic hunter–gatherers began to settle. If this is so then organized killing came late to the palette of human behaviours and is therefore not entirely innate. However, that said, killing is hard to avoid. Unless we are very strict vegans we are implicated and even then, if we garden, we are bound to destroy some form of insect life. Perhaps the answer to this conundrum is to remember that a precept is an aspiration and as such is always an ideal to aim for but not assume we will attain. In my own experience I have found that my sensitivity to the suffering of others has gradually increased as I have got older. Although I continue to occasionally eat meat, I do so less easily and at all other times halt before killing anything alive knowing that I could never create such an extraordinary being.

After killing comes stealing, harming others sexually, lying and being intoxicated. Avoiding lying has already been mentioned as a practice within the Noble Eightfold Path that leads to awakening. It includes any type of action that distorts or hides how things really are and it is this opposition to the whole purpose of the Dharma that makes it so harmful. Furthermore, a person who can readily lie is a person who has no remorse – as recent American politics has terrifyingly demonstrated – and so the path is closed to them. Interestingly, what to say or not say comes up frequently in my psychotherapeutic work. People often wonder should they say something that may be difficult for their friend or family. There is no simple answer to this but two things have guided me. The first is that the Buddha was said to never say something unless it was both true *and* useful. True or useful alone was not enough. And the second is a couple of lines from Longchenpa, a great Buddhist teacher, who gives the advice that we may want to tell our friends a truth for their own good but, though it may be true, be careful we are not placing a 'tumour in their heart'.

Stealing and doing damage to others sexually seem clear but I suspect, as with killing, what exactly they constitute to each of us individually is connected to our level of sensitivity. This is also where intoxication comes in. In Buddhism the 'three root poisons' that obscure our awakened nature are delusion, grasping and aversion. Becoming intoxicated is to intentionally delude ourselves; it obscures mindfulness and encourages not being present with things as they really are. In such a state, it is easy to believe that actions that hurt ourselves and others are not really doing so.

Around two or three hundred years after the Buddha's death, new Mahayana teachings began to appear that radically changed Buddhist ethics. Prior to this time, for all their humanity, ethical action was cut and dried – this is wholesome, this is not. However, this new teaching was more nuanced and said that under some exceptional situations those actions that were prohibited could be skilfully performed. Sometimes it was OK to apparently kill and lie, etcetera. This of course then opened the door to interpretation and the possibility of making mistakes. It also moved the understanding of acting well much closer to how most of us practise it today. My choices are based on my own understanding and values, on most things they are not set by external rules. In the West, this has enabled many philosophical explorations of what makes for ethical actions and the discovery that once we begin to think about it carefully it becomes very complicated. This may not be resolved – certainly not here – but if we move from thought and go to the wisdom of our bodies we may find that on a felt sense level we do already know – at least for us – what does harm and what is good. And one thing is clear: when I take full responsibility for my emotions – it is not someone else's fault – I immediately gain my agency and become free.

Kindness and compassion

During the years that my wife Philippa Vick and I have taught mindfulness, we have seen the pervasive presence of self-criticism and self-persecution – particularly among the women in the groups. This has been widely noticed and out of this has grown the work of Paul Gilbert on compassion-focused therapy and more generally the recognition of the importance of kindness and compassion as an essential aspect of mindfulness training and life in general. However, we also all live within a narcissistic society that easily mistakes real self-care for an obsession with the self and, if caught in this mistake, we may find ourselves living in an entirely selfish world of unsustainable self-indulgence while remaining deeply barren and unfulfilled inside.

A counter to all this is perhaps an aspiration written by the eighth-century Buddhist monk Shantideva which may be found in his profoundly influential *Way of the Bodhisattva*; it is:

> May all beings know happiness and the roots of happiness,
> May all beings be free of suffering and the roots of suffering.

These two lines (or something that contains their spirit) are used when we in meditation cultivate kindness and compassion for ourselves – we too are sentient beings! – and everyone else besides. The first line focuses on kindness – it is kind to wish happiness for others irrespective of who they are and – though hard – what they have done. The second line concerns compassion, the wish that we all may not suffer – again irrespective of whether we feel others deserve it or not. At this point someone usually asks are we saying that they should forgive someone who has hurt them very badly? The answer to this is no. This practice of loving kindness and compassion is not about forgiveness, a concept that is often caught up with our experience of Christianity. Rather, it is about wishing that the circumstances that made someone capable of hurting someone else no longer occur and that through this the hurting may come to an end. Furthermore, when we consciously grow kindness and compassion in ourselves it opens our heart and the benefits of this become a force for the good within the world generally.

Though this practice sounds perhaps a bit unrealistic or even naive it is actually extremely powerful and sometimes self-confronting. If we really try to do it we may find that we are brought into contact with the places inside ourselves where we are shut down, harbour resentments and grudges, and generally find ourselves not to be the lovely person we imagined ourselves to be. If this happens then great! We are now in touch with how things really are and it is only by bringing kindness and compassion to these dark places within ourselves, bringing presence and acceptance to whatever we find, that we will truly recognize our shared and often flawed humanity and turn the persecution of ourselves and others into a field of open, warm-hearted connection with the world. However dark things are, nothing is more powerful than love.

PRESENT WITH SUFFERING

THOUGHTS ARE NOT FACTS

I just feel I'm going crazy, my thoughts are driving me mad.

In our house in Devon I have painted one entire wall with blackboard paint and on it we chalk up telephone numbers and messages. Right across the top of it in large letters is written 'Not Necessarily So'. This is a saying from the Zen Roshi Shunryu Suzuki and it constantly counters our inclination to take what we think to be the truth.[51] It asks, do you really know that? It is a great question. Most of us just assume what we think is true, that our thoughts are facts, but once we begin to become more aware of our thought process it becomes apparent that it is frequently distorted and inaccurate. This is powerfully demonstrated by an exercise that comes from the Mindfulness-Based Cognitive Therapy course. It asks us to imagine ourselves walking along a familiar street and seeing a friend walking in the opposite direction on the other side. We raise our arm and call to them but they do not respond and continue walking. What happens then inside us? Having done this exercise with hundreds of people it turns out that we more or less have three types of reaction. A smaller group immediately think there is something wrong with the other person. Believing this they go to versions of

Being present with emptiness

'stuff you!' However, for the majority, the reaction is more about confusion, guilt, embarrassment and hurt. They feel it is somehow about them. The last group wonder if the other person is OK or, more rationally, whether they actually have been seen. This exercise which invites us to fill in the gaps with our own imagination reveals not only how readily we do so but also how what we fill the gaps with is intimately connected to our sense of who we are and our previous experiences. Those who say 'stuff you' may well be uncomfortable with the feelings of rejection and vulnerability that not being seen engenders. Protecting ourselves against these emotions, it becomes the fault of the other. The second group are put in touch with feelings of not being good enough, that there is something wrong with me and that I am unwanted. The last group splits between those of us who make things OK by being rational – a rather grown-up way of coping – and those who, having a secure sense of who they are, can afford to think of others. When, at the end of this exercise, we remind the group that we gave no indication why their greeting was not returned, it becomes apparent how much we are creating our own reality and how deeply this is embedded within us. The exercise usually evokes strong physical reactions – tightness in the chest, sickness in the stomach, shoulders braced, up and forward. Some protective, some vulnerable. Our thoughts are revealed to go down into the deep somatic memories held within our body. Past traumas are triggered and become active in the present, clouding things as they really are. And, as we have seen, the more we believe these narratives – our stories about ourselves and others – the stronger and more persuasive they become.

Cognitive Behavioural Therapy (CBT) has identified three patterns of thinking that particularly distort how things really are – they are ruminating, catastrophizing and generalizing. Thinking in these ways depletes our ability to accept ourselves just as we are with kindness and compassion and simultaneously further embeds painful ways of being. Though not a CBT therapist, I have found that within a depth psychotherapy that values mindfulness, identifying these thinking patterns is invaluable. They are the ways past hurts continue to hurt us in the present. Learning to spot and then interrupt them is an important step on the path to awareness.

Ruminating

When we ruminate we endlessly go over or round and round something that is bothering us but without any benefit. Another description of this is pointless worry. More often than not we do not even know we are doing it. It is an anxiety that occurs on the periphery of consciousness – if it were more central it would be clearer and more purposeful, properly thinking something out and coming to a conclusion. This in contrast is wearing, debilitating, it saps energy. It appears in pauses of activity, when we try to sleep and when we wake in the middle of the night. Just out of sight it lies in wait and ambushes us over and over again.

Catastrophizing

This might be considered a subset of rumination or something quite separate. Here we take what is bothering us and blow it up into a catastrophe – imagining that something is going to go very badly or be a disaster. If it is money worries, it becomes bankruptcy and penury. If it is health, it becomes immediately terminal. If it is relationships, it is violence, betrayal and abandonment. Thinking like this causes panic and we can literally trigger our own fight, flight or freeze reactions, clouding our rational judgement and flooding our system with adrenalin. We can even frighten ourselves to death.

Generalizing

Like imagining catastrophes, generalizing takes the situation, the problem, and imagines that because it has happened once it will happen again. Though similar to fantasizing disasters, I imagine it goes sideways rather than up. Not just one bad thing happening once, but it now repeating itself over and over again. Or this now having happened it will mean that other bad things will inevitably follow. Generalizing can be heard clearly in conversation and in the voice in our head – 'I'll *never* get this right', 'It's *always* going to go bad', 'Now nobody will *ever* love me'. Generalizing is the unnecessary creating of a 'forever-ness' when just one thing in the present has gone wrong.

The Two Arrows

A second approach to working with our thoughts – and by implication the emotions that permeate them – is called the 'Two Arrows' and was taught by the historical Buddha. Sharon Salzberg, one of the earliest western Insight Meditation teachers, in her book, *A Heart as Wide as the World*,[52] tells the story of how her own teacher taught her about this via a plate of chillies. For both of them the chillies were undeniably hot. However, whereas Sharon found them unbearable and imagined they may be harming her stomach, Munindraji, from his cultural perspective, experienced them as beneficial to his health. One thing sensed the same but two different reactions. The Buddha teaches about this in a discourse where he separates basic sensations from all the additional thoughts that are added to them. As a sentient human being, we are continuously inundated with sensations, some pleasant and enjoyable, others not. These we can do nothing about, there is no way to control them: chillies are simply hot. However, to these sensations we bring complex reactions, cloaking them in our previous experiences, wanting or rejecting them and being triggered into unconscious and automatic behaviours. However, although we can do nothing about the sensations themselves, the first arrow, we do have a choice about the second, our reactions. When we translate this into emotions it becomes stronger still. We all experience emotions we would rather not have. Many of us are uneasy with feeling angry or sad. Emotions such as envy or spite may be felt as deeply shameful. Here the first arrow is the anger, sadness, envy and spitefulness. These are just emotions that happen in us and that generally we have no way of preventing – it is just being human. But to these we add the additional layer of the second arrow. Creating a story about whether we should or should not have such emotions we feel angry or ashamed at ourselves for being angry or sad. We condemn ourselves as bad when we discover selfishness or the desire for revenge. None of these secondary level emotions has any real value, they just make something difficult worse. Being at war with ourselves, not accepting that what arises within us just does, does nothing to make it better. Unlike unconditional presence that greets and embraces difficult thoughts and emotions with kindness and equanimity *while not acting upon them*, the second arrow makes our wounds bigger. So much better then to accept that we are human and bring mindfulness to what we feel. Leaving it just as it is in the knowledge that, because all emotions are empty, they will change of their own accord in their own time.

That said, there is a deep addiction to the stories we tell ourselves about ourselves and others. Think of something you really believe about yourself and imagine someone entirely denying or challenging it – you are not a nice, kind person, or the opposite, you are not fundamentally bad and to blame. Most of us, hearing such challenges react defensively, reasserting our commitment to our self-beliefs. We cling to our narratives as if they are life itself. And in a way they are. We all need to have an idea of who we are and the more accurate this is the better. However, who we are is always under threat as circumstances and change undermine us. Much of the time it is as if we are fire-fighting to save our image of who we are or the vulnerabilities that lie beneath this. Defending our identity becomes a two-edged sword, at times it has saved our sanity but at others it has kept us in a small, frightened place. The message is clear; I need to treat who I am with a light touch, truth is I am always changing and who knows where this may lead.

Finally *working* with our thoughts is necessary. Thoughts are frequently deep-seated habits: wishing them away, waiting for a magic wand, will not change anything but cultivating awareness will. Whether we are catching destructive thought patterns or layers of self-punitive emotions, when we intervene with kindness and humour and stop believing our own story we begin to be freer. Not having a set position we have less to defend. Being open to the views of others and the entire spectrum of our own feelings, we begin to enjoy the sensation of learning. Not knowing something is exciting, it creates a space for unforeseen possibilities. Knowing nothing whatsoever, having a 'beginner's mind', is the most exciting of all – the vast expanse of emptiness is spontaneous potential.

MINDFULNESS

I could forget who I am.

The most important thing about the practice of mindfulness is that it enables us to be present with what we are experiencing in an open and kindly way. Nature gives us the options of being entirely identified with what we are feeling or removed and cut off. The first has us carried away by emotions, thoughts and behaviours that are sometimes destructive, finding ourselves saying and doing things that we later regret. A 'hot head' caught up on automatic pilot. The second leaves us removed from ourselves and others, not in touch, dissociated. Express it or repress it. However mindfulness offers us a third option, a middle way between the two where resting in unconditional presence offers a unique means for healing deep hurts and coming to see how things really are.

The way we teach mindfulness is derived from the earliest form that the Buddha himself taught and a later form found in several teachings, including those of the Great Perfection, a Buddhist tradition found in India and then Tibet from about the eighth century CE on.[53] Leaving the Great Perfection aside for the moment, the Buddha describes the elements of meditation in the Noble Eightfold Path. They are: Right Effort, Right Mindfulness and Right Concentration. But just before we look at them it helps to know that we can exchange the word 'Right' for 'Perfect' – it is the way in which they are most helpfully done.

Right Effort

For years I ignored this – it sounded like hard work. Now I profoundly value it as a lifesaver. It is very simple: when something unwholesome (see above) pops into my mind or has established itself as my thought process, something that is all about small contracting emotions and stories, I try to notice it and let it go. Pouf! And when something wholesome comes to mind or I am already in it, when I notice it I encourage it. Please stay! This is 'abstain from evil, cultivate the good' in action. It is amazing how accomplished we can get at this quite quickly – which is probably why I like it. However, there is a profound difference between letting go of difficult emotions and simply repressing them. A repressed emotion will return again and again and may even take a physical expression if repressed successfully. This is not the same as recognizing a favourite old chestnut or bugbear, an obsession or irritation that just aggravates us, and deciding not to go round the loop yet again. An emotion that is more of a trigger will need to be worked with in a way that our relationship to it is changed – this we will come to in the next section.

Right Mindfulness

This is the crucial part. Mindfulness, *sati*, is the keen and sustained awareness of what is happening inside and outside of me. It includes my body, sensations, emotions, thoughts and how I am behaving. It also includes my environment and interactions with other people. Most of us start off with the idea that mindfulness is about finding a relaxed state we can take a rest in, a place where we can take time out from our stressful life. Although there is an element of truth about this it is not entirely true. Mindfulness has two aspects to it. The first is that through sustained concentration – more on this in a moment – our mind begins to calm. The second is that having a calm mind enables us to see more clearly what is happening within and around us. These two, calm abiding, *shamatha*, and insight, *vipashyana*, are two interdependent parts of the one practice. An image that conveys this is holding a glass of water in which the sediment has become shaken up, making the water murky. If we continue to shake the glass, the water will remain murky but if we stop the agitation the water will clear as the sediment settles on the bottom. In the same way, if we stop agitating our mind, resting it on – for example – our breath, in time our mind will settle and give insight into all the thoughts and emotions that were swirling around it. Pema Chödrön talks about when this happens. She says we all expect our meditation to create a lovely chilled-out space but the reality is when we stop, when the water clears, what we find in the bottom is all the old rubbish that has accumulated over the years. However, this is not a disaster. Knowing what is happening in our mind, being able to remain present with some equanimity is the purpose of mindfulness. Not hiding in an artificially constructed blissful state of mind but able to be with things just as they are. Real.

Right Concentration

This returns to calming the mind. After the Buddha left home he studied with several teachers who each taught him methods of profound concentration. He discovered that the deeper and longer the concentration, the calmer he got. The practice of concentration, *samadhi*, leads – if heroically pursued – to experiences of deep absorption, *dhyana*, that create a platform of equanimity from which insight may be gained. Here we are back with not shaking the murky water. But it is also more than this. Even on a less heroic level, equanimity is acceptance. As we practise mindfulness we begin to be less at war with ourselves. We discover that we are not our thoughts or emotions, that they come and go, and it really does not matter however bad or mad they are. Sitting back in our observing awareness, we can see our 'stuff' just coming or going, stepping back from 'all about me', a space where we can let things go. A space of real kindness.

Objects of mindfulness

A note here might be useful as I have frequently found that mindfulness, as an activity, and what we are mindful of, the object of our mindfulness, easily get confused. So an object of mindfulness is what we choose to be mindful of. We can be mindful of our breath, the physical sensations found within our body, our emotions and thoughts or – most importantly – awareness itself. With perhaps the exception of awareness, our object of mindfulness is less important than our being mindfully present with it. Bringing together the combination of concentration, mindfulness and clarity, and the cultivation of acceptance, equanimity and kindness that gradually grow from their practice, is more than enough in itself but it also provides the foundation for the 'unfabricated', non-dual form of mindfulness that we will come to later.

The actual experience of all this is dependent on how much time we give it. If we decide to sit for just a few minutes, there is a distinct possibility that if we are being mindful of our breath or body sensations, our minds will begin to slow down. If we choose to sit more, the calming effect will be greater. However, in my experience, sitting for longer periods of time – as we are strongly advised to do – leads to places in which we meet ourselves more fully. This is not always comfortable. Hours can be spent starring in our own block-buster movie, haunted by humiliating memories or in losses that have us swerving away from the pain. We have peeked into Pandora's Box and what we find is what we have hidden away in there. However, this is not madness. Having learnt some acceptance we have some space. We make up fewer stories based on very little. We begin to make friends with parts of ourselves that were previously enemies. We need no longer be on the run from the places we are estranged from. We may even find some humour – I never knew until now how mad my mind was – and, on the plus side, I also had no idea I could sit with it and it be OK. In this way, mindfulness goes beyond a

Being present with emptiness

relaxation exercise and reveals its real power. It is not about improving performance but authentic being.

How to practise mindfulness of the breath

1. Sitting in a comfortable but upright position take two or three deeper and slower breaths. Let yourself know that you are now beginning your mindfulness practice. Feel the seat beneath you.

2. With your eyes either closed or open, resting your gaze on the floor about two or three metres away, place your attention on your breath – breathe naturally not trying to alter it in any way. You may choose to feel it in one of three places:
    a. In the triangle made by the top lip and nostrils. Breathing in we feel the slightly cooler air, breathing out the slightly warmer.
    b. In your chest: breathing in we feel the breath filling our lungs, breathing out emptying, then a pause and the breath breathes itself in again.
    c. In the belly: breathing in we feel the muscles expand, breathing out contract.

3. When you notice you have become distracted

PRESENT WITH SUFFERING

(which will happen within seconds), carried away by thoughts of the past and future, in a kind voice in the back of your mind name this 'thinking' and then return to the breath. Repeat with each noticed distraction. Do not let this become a war with yourself – gentle and calm. If you are getting tense just stop and let it go and then start again.

4. When we find that our concentration is struggling we may support it by naming the in and out breath in our mind in a kind and gentle voice, 'rising', 'falling' or 'in', 'out'.

Things to watch out for:

- Make sure that your chin is neither resting on your chest nor tipped up; both of these positions separate your head from your body. Check this occasionally.
- Once you have established which location of the breath you are going to be mindfully present with, do not then chop and change when your attention wanders in the hope of making it better. Stick with just one until your next meditation.
- Be kind about distraction – you are not trying to stop

thinking, you are just trying to notice when caught up in thinking and gently letting it go to return to the breath. Thus the meditation is a continuous journey between breath and *fully distracted thinking* that slowly becomes more restful and clear. This noticing of thinking and letting it go is the invaluable tool you are creating.
- Do not seek to experience an idea of what you imagine the practice should feel like. Mindfulness is not a more sublime state of mind, it is simply being present with whatever we feel.
- Mindfulness is not a relaxation exercise – it is present with whatever is happening inside and outside of us.
- During practice it is not unusual to feel emotions – sometimes strong ones that given the space come to the surface. These are not distractions. Allow them to be there and simply continue. Mindfulness embraces everything with acceptance. If you would like to work with them more closely see the section on *Feels real, not true* and the *Basic space of awareness* below. We can insert this practice of mindfulness of emotions and awareness itself into our practice of mindfulness of the breath, going between them as needed.
- And remember it is better to do this for ten minutes every day at a regular time rather now and then or

PRESENT WITH SUFFERING

when we feel stressed and needing to calm down. Dabbing at it will have no benefit at all – it is all in the constancy of the practice, forming a good habit.

If this is the first time you have tried to practise mindfulness then this may be your introduction to the pleasure of emptiness. Here emptiness reveals itself as the flow of experience – thoughts come, thoughts go, emotions arise, emotions leave. And the person who is meditating begins to find a place within themselves that is not under siege from all the chaos swirling around in the mind. A place of spacious clarity that has nothing to do with the personality, the stories about who the person is. Here we find a space in which all of this is let go. I remember the first time I really experienced this. Sitting on the sofa one day, I took a breath and realized that this was nothing to do with 'me' – a breath is just a breath. And the relief of the 'burden of me' being lifted brought tears of relief and gratitude to my eyes.

We will return in the last section to the practice of mindfulness but in a form of mindfulness that is more associated with the Great Perfection and other non-dual traditions. A form of mindfulness practice that does nothing whatsoever and is simultaneously the pinnacle of practice and the most difficult to do.

FEELS REAL, NOT TRUE

The felt sense is the space in which everything can move on.

Emotions can cause problems. As a psychotherapist people tell me about their emotions and often, while doing so, look at me with a kind of forlorn hope, wanting me to do something that will make them feel better and cause the painful emotions to go away. This is particularly so when we come to emotions that are connected to previous painful or traumatic events. When these emotions are trigged in the present we not only feel the problem now, but to this is added the emotions that were experienced in the past as well. In fact, we can easily feel like a distressed child even though we are now grown-up. Emotional reactions like this are easy to recognize because they are disproportionate to the situation. Typically, something will trigger us causing a strong emotional reaction and then some time later, once the spike of emotion has receded, we will wonder what happened – we may think, 'That wasn't me'. However, whether triggered or not, the emotions we experience are influenced and deeply rooted in our previous experiences. Our emotional past is entirely in the present. Though not always a problem, emotions do nonetheless colour the immediacy of our experience and conceal how things really are. Buddhism refers to this in unequivocal language. Conflicted emotions, *klesha*, are what obscures our radiant, awakened mind. This being so, the saying, 'feels real, but not necessarily true', is a valuable mantra.

Because of this the mindfulness courses we teach build towards becoming aware of the emotions that may be felt in our body. To be human is to have emotions and, whether we are aware of them or not, they are continuously present unless we are in deep sleep. However, emotions are tricky things. On the one hand, we are unable to place a value on things unless we have an emotional reaction or response. The neurologist and neuroscientist Antonio Damasio describes a patient who had received an injury to that part of his brain, his limbic system, that is predominantly concerned with emotion.[54] Though still entirely rational and able to think of the pluses and minuses of a situation, he was incapable of making any value judgements – to do this required an emotion. However, on the other hand, the emotions we have are almost always coloured by our past and because of this we are not reacting to what is happening now but to what has happened before. When my usually kind and loving wife yells at me my emotional reaction is that of a small boy being yelled at by his rather frightening mother. When powerful gales hammer our wooden house set high up a valley on the edge of the moor, the disquiet I feel is disproportionate to the situation. The house has stood for over a hundred years but I feel physically endangered, a feeling, as far as I can tell, that stems from early infancy. And it also works with pleasurable emotions. Advertising is full of triggers, linking a product – car, perfume, jewellery, chocolate, furniture, houses – with enjoyable situations we have all previously known or have yearned for.

In a book provocatively called *What Freud Didn't Know*, Timothy Stokes, a clinical psychologist, says if we wish to work with painful emotions, traumas that are situated in the past, it is not enough to simply recall and understand the history of what has psychologically wounded us.[55] For a different relationship to these emotions to occur it requires that we do something different when the emotions are triggered. This makes sense. The neural pathways in our brains are rather like tracks through a wood. Every time we travel down them they become more trodden in. Emotions that are repeated over and over again, accompanied by the same thoughts and behaviours simply embed themselves more deeply. To create a new pathway, making new neural connections, requires that we bring awareness to the triggered emotions *when triggered*. Recognizing we have been triggered and – as far as we are able – stepping back from the habitual thoughts and actions that accompany the trigger. This is necessary because it is only by experiencing something differently that new neural circuitry is made and new experiences become available. One of the devices that is extremely useful for working with our distorted emotional perceptions and the stories we create around them is supplied by Pema Chödrön. It is: Acknowledge, Do Something Different and Do It Again. We have slightly enhanced this so it becomes: Acknowledge, Do Something Different (go to the body) and Do It Again. This is also very similar to something developed by Tsoknyi Rinpoche which he calls the 'handshake practice'.[56]

Acknowledge

This is perhaps the most difficult step. We need to be able to recognize when a difficult emotion has been triggered. However, catching ourselves when suddenly fearful, angry or shamed is not easy because the power of the emotion itself is almost overwhelming. This is where the previous practice of mindfulness comes in. Mindfulness is a guard at the gate, our protector, and if she is awake she will clearly know when the danger turns up and bangs on the door. Through our mindfulness, insight is also accumulated and we begin to know what situations are likely to trigger us. When someone talks to us with what we hear as a certain type of authority, when a request is made that we receive as a manipulation, up pops our mantra – this feels real but it may not be true.

Do Something Different (go to the body)

For something to change we need to do something different when triggered. It is the 'when triggered' that is the important part – hard though this is. All contemporary trauma treatments now work on this principle – just going over and over what distresses us simply ingrains the hurt. We need instead to form a different relationship to the wound that is fully present but not identified. This is where we teach a variation of 'focusing'.

The creator of the focusing technique was Eugene Gendlin, an American philosopher and psychologist.[57] His research into what made psychotherapy work revealed that those of us who can feel an internal body awareness and are able to speak from this felt sense fare better than those who feel nothing while caught up in interminable stories. Gendlin defines the felt sense as a kind of inner knowledge that is not immediately available but, when focused on, can be captured by a word, phrase or image. It is within these that its meaning becomes apparent. Here it is important to distinguish between sensations that are essentially emotions and those that are simply physical sensations such as a crick in the neck or a headache. Though there is some crossover between the two, generally they are different. Gendlin says that the felt sense is not an emotion but having taught being with the felt sense to many people I am sure this is not right. Plainly what we feel in our bodies is emotion and it is this that is cloaked in meaning. When we are in touch with our felt sense it is a sensation felt within our body and, if we remain present with this sensation it will usually either quickly fade or unfold into another felt sense. When this happens, if accompanied by a kind of release or deeper insight, it is called a 'felt shift'. For instance initial anger may open more deeply into sadness or fear and by being simply present with this something changes and we find ourselves more relaxed and open. The sense or presence itself is strengthened. That said, getting a felt shift should not be the goal of focusing. Its real value is in its simple and accepting presence. In the technique that Gendlin developed to help those of us who do not focus naturally there are six steps. These are: 1. Slowing down and feeling inside. 2. Becoming conscious of the felt sense or senses. This initially will not be entirely clear. 3. Finding which word, phrase or image captures or 'resonates' with the felt sense best. 4. Checking this resonance so as to be certain. 5. Asking what is this about? It is this that may give some further insight and elicit a felt shift. 6. Receiving – whatever happens we accept it with a feeling of gratitude.

However, this sequence, which is often used to resolve problems and is used within psychotherapeutic settings, may be simplified. By dropping steps 3, 4, 5 and 6, the intention to find a resolution is let go of and instead is replaced by a practice

Being present with emptiness

of awareness where the felt sense, as simply the emotions felt within our body, becomes our object of mindfulness.

John Welwood, a psychotherapist, Buddhist and originally a research student of Gendlin's, develops this further.[58] Lifting the pure mindfulness from within the focusing technique, he observes that there are actually two types of felt shift. The first is where an emotion opens into a further emotion – a 'horizontal felt shift', and the second where the emotion opens into non-dual awareness – a 'vertical felt shift'. We may imagine this as moving through a vast house. Each door opens into another room which in turn has other doors that lead to further rooms. Emotions endlessly lead to other emotions. But just very, very occasionally we open a door and are astonished to find that we have stepped outside the building. Suddenly the confines of our person recede as we rest in a clear and spacious awareness. It is then in this way that we teach Do Something Differently (go to the body).

1. Acknowledging that you have been triggered and finding that you have a strong emotion – negative or positive – turn your attention to your body. Ask, 'Where am I feeling this?'
2. Resting your attention inside, probably principally your torso, throat and possibly head, notice where you can feel something. At first this may not be that

clear or strong – Gendlin calls this 'a fuzzy felt sense'. If there is more than one, choose the strongest. The felt sense is often very faint or subtle as it is at first just beneath the level of awareness. However, it can also be very strong and feel quite overpowering. In either case it is essential that you do not immediately fall into identification with the felt sense so that you lose your observer. It is a relationship, it requires a small distance between you and it. We feel it but are not it.

3. Having identified the location of the felt sense, just remain present with it. You are not trying to understand it, change it or make it go away. It is left exactly as it is. If in touch with something difficult it may help to breathe around or through it, creating some space and saying to oneself: 'It's OK to be with this.' This is difficult to do. The temptation is very strong to flip back into lots of thoughts about the felt sense and the story around it. If you have practised mindfulness you will recognize this as just thinking. Drop this as soon as you spot it and return to mindfulness of the felt sense. With practice this becomes much easier.

4. All emotions are empty which is to say they change – more emotion or they simply fade away. Not

adding any story, not adding a second arrow of further reactive emotions causes them to pass more quickly. Research suggests – almost unbelievably – that a spike of intense emotion lasts no more than 90 seconds if not repeatedly renewed by the thoughts associated with it. When awareness of the felt sense goes, if meditating return to the breath or a 'doing nothing' meditation, or if during daily events continue with what you were doing.

Do it Again

Though a single attempt to be present with our emotions is valuable, to make any real difference we must repeat it again and again. Our neural pathways become progressively more set the older we get so it takes ardent application to create new ones. However, the good news is that we now know our brains have a greater degree of plasticity then was previously thought and change is a real possibility. The psychologist Donald Hebb, as early as 1949, had recognized that 'neurons that fire together wire together'. One implication of this is if we commit ourselves to create a different relationship to our emotions and thoughts we will slowly but surely make new pathways.

Finally, this method may not be for all. It requires that

we have the ability to go towards powerful and often painful emotions and not simply get swamped by them which may then re-traumatize us. If we are a clinician, we will know that the defences of those we work with are important – they have after all probably saved their sanity – and will know not to push. If we are doing this alone, for ourselves, then our own defences will helpfully kick in if it gets too much and feels overwhelming. But again, it is important not to push and if we really come up against something difficult seek professional help. When triggered it is usually connected to the character styles that we visited in A Meditation on the Pain of Emptiness. Core wounds lie behind most of our emotional reactions – my fear of the wind may be traced back to sensing the world as a dangerous place when tiny: a baby fearing annihilation. Core wounds similarly may sit behind feelings of being unloved and alone, being swallowed up in relationships, being vulnerable, being oppressed, being out of control or not seen and heard. All of these have taken years to install and will take a great amount of time, care, kindness and some humour to reverse. That said, this is an extraordinary way of working with emotions that may have caused us a great deal of suffering throughout our lives. It has a truly transformative power. Focusing and this adapted form take the ideas about emptiness that we visited in a Meditation on the Delight of Emptiness and put them into action. Emotions, as are thoughts, are always changing and are dependent upon many factors. By letting go of the stories that surround and maintain them, their fluid and transparent nature becomes apparent and the luminous mind they are an expression of becomes more accessible.

THE BASIC SPACE OF AWARENESS

This self-awareness is naturally free from the very first
How amazing that it is liberated by just resting at ease in whatever happens!

Shabkar Tsokdruk Rangdrol

During the first thousand years of the unfolding of the Buddha's teaching, the understanding of consciousness evolved. At first it was understood as something that was dependent on the stimulation of the senses or the movement of the mind. When things happen I am conscious of them and when they are not happening I am not. In this way consciousness was just the same as everything else – its existence relied on other factors. However, within the Buddha's teaching lay the hint of something that would become the most profound insight of later Buddhism – the Buddha said that the mind is 'brightly shining'.[59, 60] This insight grew with time.⁶¹ It became associated with the idea of a buddha-nature, the awakened mind that already exists within us, and in the non-dual systems of Dzogchen and Mahamudra found in Tibet, with the ground of being.⁶²,⁶³ The basic space of awareness, *rigpa*, that was not dependent for its existence on other factors, a naked and uncontrived awareness that was empty, lucid and an unconstrained expanse of compassionate energy. Although early Buddhism had largely described its ultimate truth in the negative – things are always changing, this is true of us also and this feels like a bumpy ride – here the description became transformed. The ground of being, in which everything arises, primordially pure and spontaneously present awareness, when directly experienced, utterly uncloaked, is the Great Bliss, *mahasukha*.

Doing something and nothing

With this revolution also came a change in the way meditation was understood, no longer solely about renunciation or transformation, it became a path of uncovering or disclosing what is already here. A path of 'self-liberation' where thoughts, if left entirely alone, disperse of their own accord. Joseph Goldstein, one of the first American Insight Meditation teachers, describes this shift in his book *Mindfulness*, as 'fabricated and unfabricated mindfulness', and Shinzen Young, an American Zen teacher, calls it quite simply a 'Doing

Being present with emptiness

Nothing Meditation'[64]. Put plainly, doing something meditations require effort and the intention to arrive somewhere or achieve something – to calm the mind, to see things as they really are – but now a new instruction emerged that was to relax and do nothing whatsoever. Why? Because any attempt to create or improve resting in intrinsic awareness, the non-dual nature of the mind, immediately obscures any possibility of doing so. For this special insight to occur we need to do the almost impossible – let our trying to change and improve things go and surrender into presence.

Different Buddhist traditions teach 'doing nothing' meditation practices in different ways. Some openly offer a means to glimpse intrinsic awareness.[65] Others, including Dzogchen, the Great Perfection, require it to be taught by someone who is part of a lineage of teachers who have been practising it from its inception. This said, investigating YouTube will reveal Tibetan Lamas and others who, believing in the value of doing so, openly share these types of 'pointing-out instructions'. Some years back we began to gently introduce to the groups we teach widely available versions of this practice, offering them as something we valued and that may be of value to others. Borrowing initially from Shinzen Young and his instructions on YouTube and then adding others as we discovered and practised them for ourselves.[66] Several examples of these doing nothing meditations and how to 'practise' them may be found below.

All doing nothing meditations begin with doing something – calming the mind. Having a calm mind that is neither drowsy nor agitated provides a foundation for what follows; without it the mind will quickly skip off and the doing nothing meditation will simply become straightforward doing nothing whatsoever other than being distracted. Calming meditations come in two forms – with and without an object. We have already met an example of the with an object type of practice earlier in the mindfulness section where instructions for mindfulness of breathing are included. Here the object was the breath. Apart from the breath, other objects of mindfulness have traditionally included simple objects such as a coloured circle or single letters such as an A. Slightly more challenging are calming practices that are without an object as these, being more formless, are heading in the direction of doing nothing. An example of this type of objectless practice is where we rest our attention on a visualized letter A in the space before us or, more formless still, rest our attention on the space around us, broadening and softening our focus and, in a relaxed and gentle way, being present with whatever arises to our senses. Though profound, and certainly not easy, these practices remain dualistic in that there remains an observer and what is observed. For this to take the next and final step, the nature of these two must be recognized as essentially the same – both are awareness.

Having established our calm base through mindfulness of breathing, or a similar 'doing something' practice, here are several doing nothing meditations that may quite spontaneously offer a glimpse of the basic space of awareness. But a word of warning – this awareness is not created or achieved; better to think of it as a visitor who may arrive by their own devices. All we are doing here is getting out of the way should the visitor come – this way we are freed of the impediment of expectation.

This first practice is derived from various instructions I have received personally. Approach it with curiosity and try not to be disappointed or discouraged if your experience does not match your expectations. When you sit, this is something that just clicks instantly or it does not. Trying hard is to no avail! Even when we think we have glimpsed the basic space of awareness once, this does not guarantee that it will not be a long time before the next glimpse. Patience and kindness.

The basic practice

Sit facing a blank wall or a cloudless sky (opposite to the sun), your body and mind entirely relaxed but not collapsed.

PRESENT WITH SUFFERING

Consciously bring yourself back from being immersed in thoughts into awareness of the experience of this present moment. Here, now.

Rest your open eyes just above your visual horizon – they are not sharply focused but rather softly take in a wide arc of vision. If they start to blur or tear up relax them again. We are not staring at anything.

Now notice your own awareness and then do nothing. In the moment you do this you may glimpse that awareness has nothing at its centre, there is no 'you' there. It is a space that is nonetheless aware. Do not correct or alter your experience in any way at this point. Here awareness knows itself without thought. Rest in this effortlessly.

When you find you have left spacious awareness (maybe almost immediately) and have returned to present moment awareness (subject and object) or have become identified with your thoughts, just notice this, let it go and start again. Similarly, if you feel that something rather fixed or spacey is happening, break this state and start again. Remember this is not an altered state of consciousness; it is the 'natural state'.

Continue in this way, back and forth, throughout your entire session.

The next one was given to us by a mindfulness teacher in Oxford – so we call it the 'Oxford' practice. The teacher said those who practised it sometimes found themselves spontaneously resting in the basic space of awareness.

The 'Oxford' practice

Begin by being mindfully present with your breath. When things have quietened down, open your awareness to include your entire body. Whatever you experience, leave it as it is. Do not try to understand, change or improve what you are experiencing – it is fine as it is. Do nothing. Then when you notice you have been carried away by thoughts, return to the breath for a few minutes and then start again.

Repeat this cycle throughout the entire practice time.

The third practice comes from Pema Chödrön and is interesting as it incorporates a very pure doing nothing practice within something that has more form. She says that her own teacher initially gave it as a doing nothing meditation but then added a couple of things to do when he realized people were struggling.[67]

> Relax as it is
>
> Start with the mind open and relaxed. If thoughts distract then let them go and return to the open and relaxed state of mind.
>
> To help resting in the open and relaxed mind, place a small amount of attention on each out-breath – maybe 25 per cent – do not let this become just watching the breath. The breath is merely to help us rest in the present. When we breathe in we do nothing in particular.
>
> And lastly, if very distracted we can name the distraction 'thinking' in a kind voice, at the back of our mind.
>
> Here the basic instruction is – just stay – do not try to alter anything, be present within your experience without judgement, kind and accepting.

Being present with emptiness

Things to watch out for

- If you are used to meditating with closed eyes do not revert back to this. Eyes open, soft focus, resting just above the horizon.
- Avoid a rigid 'meditation position' – remain comfortable, relaxed but without fidgeting; stay still.
- Do not – however tempting – practise with one eye on whether you are experiencing the basic space of awareness or not. This cannot be said strongly enough: it is completely and utterly impossible for the cognitive mind to answer this question. When you are it is completely obvious, but only the experience can confirm it.
- Likewise trying hard is an impediment. Sit regularly but with a light touch. Be indifferent to whatever happens. Avoid grasping.
- Doing nothing meditations are not an altered state of consciousness – if you sense that you have entered one, maybe a bit spaced-out or stiff, break it and just relax back into normal.
- You will have many doubts whether you have had a glimpse of this or not. These may cause attempts to manipulate or 'improve' the method of the practice in some way. Doing this will help in no way whatsoever.
- And remember, it is always simpler than we think. If

you have an idea of what it might be like, it is not. Drop it.

Research reveals that many people experience 'spiritual openings', often quite unexpectedly and without any intention. Frequently not understood or even wanted, we usually know something different has happened. I believe I had my first glimpse of the basic space of awareness over 30 years ago when sitting with my wife in an empty cafe on the island of Gozo in the Mediterranean. Spontaneously we both found ourselves completely relaxed and at ease. All the sights, sounds, smells and sensations of being there remained the same, or perhaps were just a little more vivid, as did our awareness of each other across the table – it was not so much an altered state as just being entirely and effortlessly present. A spacious awareness, not pointedly fixed on anything, in which thoughts still existed but, being on the periphery of this awareness, were not followed and so they dissolved of their own accord. Entirely natural and oddly ordinary. Of course this is impossible to describe and the description itself is double-edged because, while it attests the reality of intrinsic awareness, it also gives an idea that could easily mislead. This event continued for some time until we decided to leave and go for a walk, but while we sat there it was timeless. Many years passed without me thinking of it again, and then after years of attempting to 'do' doing nothing meditations, I perhaps began to care and try less and in that opening found what I had previously known on Gozo again. The secret of this most profound way of being with ourselves is a very light touch, almost indifference, and allowing whatever experience we are having to unfold – being present with things as they really are. The basic space of awareness, the background silence, is already here now. It has never gone. Once we know its flavour, recognition becomes easier and with each further recognition, confidence grows. So, how long does this take? A lifetime!

THE IMPOSSIBILITY OF COMING TO AN END

Your joy is your sorrow unmasked.
Kahlil Gibran

A few years back I was teaching a class at the Sharpham Barn Retreats in Devon, in the UK. Driving there I listened to a terrible programme on the radio and, from what I heard, I arrived in a place of black despair. This world seems so horrible at times and we are so persistently stupid and cruel. I shared these feelings with the retreatants – I said that sometimes I doubted the Buddhist teaching and could find no refuge within it. It too could feel bleak and empty. However, to my surprise it came back to me later that many felt this was the most inspiring talk on the Dharma they had ever received. I guess it was at least honest.

My relationship to the Dharma is as a student and a pretty poor one at that. This is not closet vanity. Having sat on my bottom and looked into Pandora's Box the experience is both salutary and humbling. And it is the same with a long period of psychotherapy – if it has worked then we are left with few illusions about ourselves. I am a flawed human being struggling to get it right. This piece started off with an inventory of the states of mind that, each in their own way, could be described as empty – emptiness as all forms of suffering. If we are to be honest with ourselves, even if we are a fully paid-up meditator, this is the way we frequently feel. And yet this is also the starting point. We do not start out by putting what hurts us behind us, we start out by turning round and being present with what we find. Not dressed up as something special, but just as it is. And this must include the recognition that presence is in itself very difficult to find and much of our time we are simply enmeshed within our own delusions and misery. Furthermore, if we consider ourselves to be meditators or Buddhists who 'should know better', then what we find may also contain a generous dollop of additional guilt.

So what I have written here is permission to be truthful with ourselves. If Buddhism is about being present with how things really are, then we are allowed to – we must – recognize the existence of the unhappiness of our ordinary emotional emptiness first. Doing so is an act of astonishing kindness and compassion. It recognizes our shared humanity: that beneath the superficial differences we are very much the same. We all wish to be happy and not sad and for any hope of this it will be necessary to slow and then stop being at war with who we already are. Acceptance, which is not the same as just putting up with things, is required, warts and all. Acceptance is trusting emptiness to change.

Too depressing?

Well maybe, but something different is paradoxically also very near. Staying with the theme of how things really are, still closer observation reveals that the problems caused by our usual perception of things being distinct from each other and truly existing ease when we really take on that, in reality, appearances are entirely contingent and transitory. That the boundaries between one thing and another are quite literally all in the imagination. Another way to put this is that everything is awareness – the deepest insight of the Great Perfection and other similar Buddhist traditions. In awareness, the perceiver, perceiving and what is perceived are all one. There is only awareness and in this sense it is awareness that is the ground of being.

Making this more than a mere idea begins with taking ourselves less seriously – by getting over ourselves, finding a lighter touch, having a 'mere' self. Remembering thoughts are not facts, and emotions, while feeling undoubtedly real, may still not necessarily be true, are means by which we may do this. Going to the wisdom of the body and seeing in its mirror how mental states, when not cosseted and identified with, are fleeting is another. Stories are just stories, our narrative, while all-consuming is still two-dimensional. And yes, it takes time to really feel this transparency but then perhaps it should – all really good things do take time to achieve.

Many years ago a person who was in psychotherapy with me repeated a disastrous mistake yet again. She liked to think of her psychotherapy as an alchemical flask in which transformations occurred. Now, in her mind her mistake had broken the flask, destroying all she had previously achieved and she was distraught. However, she brightened when I reminded her that alchemical flasks come in crates of a dozen and she could just have another one and start again. There are always endings and new beginnings – and then everything is just one cloth – it is what emptiness is all about.

Glossary

Advaita Vedanta School of Hindu philosophy associated with Adi Shankara (788–820 CE). In many respects very similar to the non-dual teachings of Dzogchen and Mahamudra found in Buddhism.

Acknowledge, Do Something Different, Do it Again Pema Chödrön's memory device to help develop presence.

alaya-vijnana See storehouse consciousness.

Asanga and Vasubandhu The two brothers associated with the Yogachara school of Buddhist philosophy founded in the fourth century CE.

anutpada Having no origin – term pointing to the atemporal buddha-nature.

background silence Term used by the Advaita Vedanta teacher Jean Marc Mantel to describe intrinsic awareness.

basic space of awareness Term used by the Buddhist master Longchen Rabjampa to describe intrinsic awareness.

bodhisattva One who has committed themselves to delivering all sentient beings from the suffering of birth, old age, sickness and death.

Brightly shining mind Term used by the Buddha to describe the luminous clarity of the mind realized in meditation when not obscured by thoughts and emotions.

Buddha-nature – *tathagatagarbha* The insight that each person has the potential for awakening within them. This awakened nature is not created; being already present it need only be uncovered.

Calm abiding – *shamatha* One of the two elements of mindfulness – a calm mind gains access to insight.

Chan School of Chinese Buddhism that becomes Zen in Japan. 'Chan' comes from the Sanskrit word *dhyana* meaning meditation.

Chittamatra See Mind Only.

conflicted emotions – *klesha* Principally the three root poisons of delusion, greed and aversion.

conventional truth In contrast to ultimate truth. The way we normally experience things partitioned into ourselves and everything else which is perceived as really existing.

Dharma The teaching of the Buddha and Buddhism as a whole.

dharmas Fleeting physical and mental events that, rather like atoms, are considered the 'basic stuff' or fundamental building blocks of experience.

Glossary

dhyana Meditation – leading to a state of perfect equanimity and awareness.

Doing nothing meditation Term referring to effortlessly resting in the nature of mind, intrinsic awareness.

duhkha Unsatisfactoriness, discontent, suffering in all its forms.

Dzogchen – Great Perfection Eighth-century CE Tibetan teaching that cultivates and establishes non-dual intrinsic awareness, *rigpa*. With Mahamudra, it is considered to be the pinnacle of Tibetan Buddhist teaching.

emptiness Complex term having many nuanced meanings that translates the Sanskrit word *sunyata*. Essentially refers to the nature of 'how things really are', the realization of which is the key Buddhist concern.

empty self The Buddha's description of each of the five skandhas that he investigated during his meditations. The point being that he found nothing eternal at the core of his being – no soul, spirit or divine true self. Not to be translated as 'no self' or 'no ego'.

felt sense The sensation of the emotions felt in the body that may give access to a deeper felt insight. Now frequently used interchangeably with interception or proprioception.

felt shift Staying with a felt sense it may open further into either a horizontal felt shift or vertical felt shift. The first further emotions, the latter non-dual, intrinsic awareness.

Five Precepts Taken by lay Buddhists – to not kill, steal, lie, misuse others sexually and become intoxicated.

focusing Method developed by Eugene Gendlin, an American philosopher and psychologist, that revolves around recognizing the felt sense.

generosity – *dana* The foundation of the Buddhist path.

Great Bliss – *mahasukha* The experience of resting in non-dual intrinsic awareness.

handshake practice Being present with difficult emotions felt within the body. Term coined by Tsoknyi Rinpoche and similar to focusing.

Heart Sutra Popular seventh-century CE Mahayana Buddhist Perfection of Wisdom sutra that contains the famous line, 'Form is emptiness, emptiness is form'.

insight – *vipashyana* One of the two elements of mindfulness – having a calm mind we gain access into the insight of 'how things really are'. It is only insight that facilitates awakening.

Glossary

Jataka Tales Tales of the Buddha's previous lives prior to becoming a Buddha.

klesha See conflicted emotions.
karuna Compassion.

Madhyamaka See Middle Way.
Mahamudra (Great Seal) Buddhist teaching that originates in eighth-century CE India that cultivates and establishes non-dual intrinsic awareness, *rigpa*. With Dzogchen considered to be the pinnacle of Tibetan Buddhist teaching.
maitri Loving kindness, unconditional friendliness.
merit An accumulation of good karma. Awakening is made possible through the accumulation of merit and wisdom.
mindfulness See *sati*.
Mind Only Alternative name for the Yogachara school of Mahayana philosophy. Makes the point that all we experience is our own mind.
Middle Way The middle way between things neither existing nor not existing, a school of Mahayana philosophy founded in the first-century CE by Nagarjuna.

Nagarjuna Philosopher monk from southern India, approached emptiness through logic and created the Mahayana Buddhist Middle Way philosophy.

Glossary

nature of mind Dzogchen term meaning the intrinsic awareness that is empty, clear and compassionate. See *rigpa*.

nirvana The occurrence of awakening, enlightenment.

objects of mindfulness Things we are mindful of – our breath, physical sensations found within our body, our emotions and thoughts and – most importantly – awareness itself.

pointing out instructions A Dzogchen initiation that reveals the nature of mind, non-dual, intrinsic awareness.

Right Effort, Right Mindfulness and Right Concentration The three aspects of the Buddhist Noble Eightfold path that pertain to meditation.

rigpa The Dzogchen definition of naked and uncontrived intrinsic awareness that is empty, lucid and an unconstrained expanse of compassionate energy. How things really are. Our buddha-nature, the basic space of awareness.

samadhi A prolonged state of meditative absorption that results from the deep and sustained practice of calm abiding. Through *samadhi* insight is gained.

samsara The world of delusion and all types of suffering.

sangha The community of Buddhist practitioners.

sati (mindfulness) The keen and sustained awareness of what is happening inside and outside of me.

self-liberation A Dzogchen term that describes how thoughts simply dissolve when no longer identified with or followed. This is what happens when we practise a 'not doing' meditation.

shamatha See calm abiding.

Shunryu Suzuki Roshi Extremely loved and revered Zen master, author of *Zen Mind, Beginners Mind*, died 1971.

shunyata See emptiness.

sila (morality) Three aspects of the Buddhist noble eightfold path – right speech, action and livelihood.

six perfections – *paramita* Generosity, morality, patience, diligence, meditative concentration and wisdom.

skandhas **– 'five heaps'** *or aggregates* Sensations, feelings, thoughts, volitions and consciousness – the five components that make up the entirety of each person.

storehouse consciousness – *alaya-vijnana* One of the signature ideas found within the Yogachara school of Buddhist Mahayana philosophy that describes the deepest layer of consciousness that carries all the karmic imprints that condition our personal experiences.

Glossary

tathata (suchness or thusness) The precognitive experience that knows how things really are before they have been cognitively identified. Being utterly in the moment, fresh and open.

tathagatagarbha See buddha-nature.

three natures One of the signature ideas found within the Yogachara school of Buddhist Mahayana philosophy that distinguishes between awakened and deluded perception.

Two Arrows Teaching given by the Buddha that distinguishes between unavoidable experiences and those that we add to them that make them worse.

ultimate truth In contrast to conventional or relative truth that sees things as really existing, the ultimate truth is emptiness. Empty – transitory and contingent – is how things really are.

vipashyana See insight.

Yogachara See Yoga Practice School.

Yoga Practice School School of Buddhist Mahayana philosophy founded by the brothers Asanga and Vasubandhu during the fourth century CE. Explores how our perception is coloured by previous experiences.

Glossary

Zen Japanese school of Buddhism – two principal schools, Soto which values 'just sitting' and Rinzai which values *koan* meditations.

Endnotes

1. J. Bowlby, *Attachment and Loss* (1971) Penguin.
2. D. W. Winnicott, *Playing and Reality* (2005) Routledge.
3. www.acat.me.uk
4. https://plumvillage.org
5. M. Epstein, *Advice Not Given: A Guide to Getting Over Yourself* (2017) Penguin Press.
6. E. Kübler-Ross, *On Death and Dying* (1969) Macmillan.
7. Francis Weller, *The Wild Edge of Sorrow* (2015) North Atlantic Books.
8. https://buddhiststories.wordpress.com
9. J. Didion, *The Year of Magical Thinking* (2005) Vintage.
10. Claude Anshin Thomas, *At Hell's Gate* (2006) Shambhala.
11. Bessel van der Kolk, *The Body Keeps the Score* (2014) Viking.
12. Bessel van der Kolk, *Traumatic Stress* (2007) Guilford Press.
13. https://sensorimotorpsychotherapy.org
14. www.heartmath.org
15. E. Wilde McCormick, *Surviving Breakdown* (1997) Vermillion.
16. T. S. Eliot, *East Coker* (1936) Faber & Faber.
17. James Hillman, *The Thought of the Heart and the Soul of the World* (1981) Spring Publications.
18. Francis Weller, *The Wild Edge of Sorrow* (2015) North Atlantic Books.
19. James Hillman, *The Thought of the Heart and the Soul of the World* (1981) Spring Publications.
20. www.heartmath.org
21. James Lynch, *The Broken Heart: The Medical Consequences of Loneliness* (1977) Basic Books.
22. M. Friedman and R. Rosenman, *Type A Behaviour and Your Heart* (1974) Fawcett.

Endnotes

23 Mark Kidel, *The Heart Has Reasons* (1991) Channel 4.
24 E. Wilde McCormick, *The Heart Attack Recovery Book* (1987) HarperCollins.
25 Pema Chödrön, *Start Where You Are: A Guide to Compassionate Living* (1994) Shambhala.
26 C. S. Lewis, *A Grief Observed* (1961) Faber & Faber.
27 Linda Hartley, www.lindahartley.co.uk/blog.html
28 Brian Clark, *Can You Hear Me at the Back?* (1979) Amber Lane Press.
29 Thich Nhat Hanh, *Call Me by My True Names* (1999) Parallax Press.
30 L. Rosenberg, *Breath by Breath* (1998) Shambhala Classics.
31 C. Feldman, *Compassion* (2005) Rodmell Press.
32 C. Germer, *The Mindful Path to Self-Compassion* (2009) Guildford Press.
33 John Weir Perry, *The Self in Psychotic Process* (1987) University of California Press.
34 Marie Cardinale, *The Words to Say It* (1984) Van Vactor & Goodheart.
35 Eugene Gendlin, *Focussing* (1988) Bantam Books.
36 Christopher Bollas *The Shadow of the Object* (1987) Routledge.
37 Grace Andren, *Speaking in Tears: The Poetry in Grief* (2018) AnCor Press.
38 Andy Harkin, 'Mind the Gap: Moving from Brain to Body' (2016) TEDX Talks
39 www.stillwatermpc.org
40 Stephen M. Johnson, *Character Styles* (1994) W. W. Norton & Company.
41 Isabella Tree, *Wilding: The Return of Nature to a British Farm* (2019) Picador.
42 Peter Wohlleben, *The Hidden Life of Trees* (2017) William Collins.
43 Thich Nhat Hanh, *The Other Shore: A New Translation of the Heart Sutra* (2014) Parallax Press.
44 Shunryu Suzuki, *Zen Mind, Beginner's Mind* (1986) Weatherhill.
45 Peter Harvey, *An Introduction to Buddhism: Teachings, History and Practices* (2013) Cambridge University Press

Endnotes

46 Sharon Salzberg, *A Heart as Wide as the World* (1999) Shambhala Publications.
47 Bessel van der Kolk, *The Body Keeps the Score: Mind, Brain and Body in the Transformation of Trauma* (2015) Penguin.
48 Nigel Wellings, Dzogchen, Who's Who and What's What in the Great Perfection, (2021) unpublished manuscript.
49 Rick Hanson, *The Buddha's Brain* (2009) New Harbinger Publications.
50 Matthieu Ricard, *Altruism: The Power of Compassion to Change Yourself and the World* (2015) Little, Brown & Company.
51 Shunryu Suzuki, *Zen Mind, Beginner's Mind* (1986) Weatherhill.
52 Sharon Salzberg, *A Heart as Wide as the World* (1999) Shambhala Publications.
53 Nigel Wellings, *Why Can't I Meditate? How to get your mindfulness practice on track* (2015) Piatkus.
54 Antonio Damasio, *The Feeling Of What Happens: Body, emotion and the making of consciousness* (2000) Vintage; Reprint Edition.
55 Timothy Stokes, *What Freud Didn't Know: A Three-step Practice for Emotional Well-Being Through Neuroscience and Psychology* (2010) Rutgers University Press.
56 Tsoknyi Rinpoche, https://pundarika.uk/beautiful-monsters-and-handshake-practice (accessed 2021).
57 Eugene Gendlin, *Focusing-Oriented Psychotherapy: A Manual of the Experiential Method* (1998) Guilford Press.
58 John Welwood, *Toward a Psychology of Awakening: Buddhism, Psychotherapy, and the Path of Personal and Spiritual Transformation* (2002) Shambhala Publications.
59 Bhikkhu Anālayo, *Satipatthana Meditation: A Practice Guide* (2018) Windhorse Publications.
60 Peter Harvey, *The Selfless Mind, Personality, Consciousness and Nirvana in Early Buddhism* (1995) Routledge Curzon.
61 Joseph Goldstein, *One Dharma* (2002) Harper San Francisco.
62 Tsoknyi Rinpoche, *Fearless Simplicity, The Dzogchen Way of Living Freely in a Complex World* (2003) Rangjung Yeshe Publications.

Endnotes

63 Namkhai Norbu Rinpoche, *The Crystal and the Way of Light: Sutra, Tantra and Dzogchen* (1986) Routledge and Kegan Paul.
64 Joseph Goldstein, *Mindfulness: A Practical Guide to Awakening* (2013) Sounds True.
65 Loch Kelly, *Shift Into Freedom, The Science and Practice of Open-Hearted Awareness* (2015) Sounds True.
66 Shinzen Young, Do Nothing Meditation (2011) YouTube.com
67 Pema Chödrön, *When Things Fall Apart* (1990) Shambhala.

Index

absorption 142–143
abuse 29–30, 128
acceptance 9–10
acknowledge 151–152
'active waiting' 35–36
ADHD (attention deficit hyperactivity disorder) 90–91
Advaita Vedanta 118
advertising 150–151
alaya-vijnana (storehouse consciousness) 109–111
Altruism (Ricard) 126–127
Amaravati Buddhist Monastery 74–75
American Insight Meditation 160–161
amygdala 108, 110–111
Andren, G. 67
anger 9–10, 30–31, 40, 46–47
angina 50–51
anutpada 106–107
anxiety 6, 40, 48–49
Arnhem, the Netherlands 70–71
Asanga (Buddhist monk) 109
At Hell's Gate (Thomas) 27
atman (the self) 95–96
attachment 3–20
attention deficit hyperactivity disorder (ADHD) 90–91
aversion 128
avoidant attachment 6
awakening 101–102, 111–113, 127–128
awareness 36, 73, 74–75, 114–115, 118, 159–169

background silence 118–119
Baltimore Penitentiary 74
bargaining 9–10
Barnard, C. 41
basic practice 163–165
basic space of awareness 159–169
being present with emptiness 117–131
bereavement 21–37, 61–63
bodhisattva 101, 124–126, 130
Bollas, C. 66–67
borderline personality disorder 89
Bowlby, J. 5–6, 10
Brahman (reality of universe) 95–96
brain 43, 107–113, 121–122, 126–127, 151–152, 157–158
breakdown 33–35
Breath by Breath (Rosenberg) 56
breathing 27–28, 36, 48–49, 61–75, 145–146, 162
Brightly shining mind 159–160
Buckle, J. 24–25
buddha (Three Jewels of Buddhism) 18
buddha-nature 159–160
Call Me by My True Names (Thich Nhat Hanh) 55, 68–69
calm abiding 141–142
Can you hear me at the back? (Clark) 54
Cardiac Department at Charing Cross 48
Cardinale, M. 65
catastrophizing 135

Index

Chan School of Buddhism 115
change, duhkha of 82–83
Character Styles (Johnson) 87–89
Chittamatra *see* Mind Only
Chödrön, P. 49, 61, 65, 122–123, 142, 151–152, 166–167
Clark, B. 54
Cognitive Analytic Therapy (CAT) 7, 17–18
Cognitive Behavioural Therapy (CBT) 132–134
collective unconscious 110–111
colourlessness 71–72
coming to an end, impossibility of 169–172
Compassion 55, 57–60, 114–115, 118–119, 129–131, 159–169
Compassion (Feldman) 57–58
concentration 140, 142–143
conditioned existence, duhkha of 82–83
conflicted emotions (*klesha*) 128
confusion 132–133
conventional truth 104–106
Corbins, H. 42
core emotional pain 17–18
core wounds 158–159
coronary spasm 48–49
courage 53–55
Damasio, A. 150–151
dana (giving) 122–126
delusion 128
denial 9–10
depression 9–10, 40, 89
despair and disorganization 10
dharma (Three Jewels of Buddhism) 18
dharmas 102–103
dhyana (absorption) 142–143
Didion, J. 21

diligence 125–126
disorganized attachment 6
Do It Again 151–152, 157–159
Do Something Different (go to the body) 151–152, 153–157
'doing something and nothing' meditation 114–115, 160–161, 168–169
duhkha 80, 82–83
Dzogchen (Great Perfection) 114–115, 159–160, 161–162
East Coker (Eliot) 35–36
effort (Noble Eightfold Path) 140–141
Eliot, T. S. 35–36
embarrassment 71–72, 132–133
emotions 17–18, 39–60, 61–75, 84–85, 86–87, 128, 149–159
empathy *see* compassion
emptiness 77–172
 basic space of awareness 159–169
 being present with 117–131
 empty self 95–100
 feels real, not true 149–159
 happy relations with the world 119–131
 impossibility of coming to an end 169–172
 mindfulness 139–148
 Present Past 107–113
 River of Change 100–107
empty self 95–100
Engaged Buddhism 18
Epstein, M. 9–10, 16–17
ethics 119–131
exhaustion 33–35, 44–45, 48–49
fabricated mindfulness 160–161
feeling empty 84–85
feels real, not true 149–159
Feldman, C. 57–58

Index

felt sense 118–119
felt shift 66, 154–155
fight or flight 30–31
Five Precepts 118–119, 126–129
fluidity/rhythms of movement 68–69
focusing 153–155
forgiveness 130–131
Freidman, - 44
gates of grief (Weller) 10–11, 15–16, 28
Gendlin, E. 66, 153–155
generalizing 135–136
generosity 118–119, 122–126
Germer, C. 58–60
Gibran, K. 169
Gilbert, P. 129–130
Goldstein, J. 160–161
Gotami, K. 11–13
grasping 128
Great Bliss 160
Great Perfection 114–115, 159–160, 161–162
greed 128
grief 8–17, 28, 40–41
Grief Observed (Lewis) 50
guilt 29–30, 132–133
'handshake practice' 152
Hanson, R. 121–122
happy relations with the world 119–131
Harkin, A. 68–69
Hartley, L. 52–53
Harvey, P. 105–106
heart 39–60
The Heart Attack Recovery Book (self-help book) 47–48
heart attacks 45–49
'heart brain' 43
The Heart Has its Reasons (Kidel) 47

Heart Sutra 79, 101–103
A Heart as Wide as the World (Salzberg) 136
Hebb, D. 157–158
The Hidden Life of Trees 100–101
Hillman, J. 41–42, 64
hippocampus 110–111
histrionic wounds 89
horizontal felt shift 155
human function curves 33–37
'hurry sickness' 49
hyperventilation 48–49
illusion 111–113, 115–116
impermanence and attachment 3–20
impossibility of coming to an end 169–172
insight 141–142
Institute of Heart Math 34, 43
Jataka Tales 124–125
jiva (divine spark) 95–96
Johnson, S. 87–89
Jung, C. G. 41–42, 81, 110–111
karuna see Compassion
Kidel, M. 47
kindness and compassion 118–119, 129–131
klesha see conflicted emotions
Kornfield, J. 16
Kübler-Ross, E. 9–10
Laity, A. 19–20
Lewis, C. S. 50
limbic system 108
living in the moment 72–75
loneliness 44, 71–72
Longchenpa (Buddhist teacher) 128
loss 21–37, 61–63
loving kindness and compassion (*maitri*) 17–18, 55–56, 73, 118–119, 129–131

Index

lungs 48–49
lying 127–128
Lynch, J. 44
'M' Technique (Buckle) 24–25
Madhyamaka *see* Middle Way
Mahamaya (Mother of Buddha) 93–94
Mahamudra (Great Seal) 114–115, 159–160
mahasukha (Great Bliss) 160
Mahayana Buddhism 101–102, 128–129
maitri 17–18, 55–56, 73
Mantel, J. M. 118
masochistic wounds 88–89
meditation 81–116
meditation on emptiness 95–116
meditative concentration 125–126
memory 28–32, 110–112, 133–134
merit 122–125
Middle Way 103–104, 106–107, 111–112, 115–116
mind the gap process 61–75
Mind the Gap (Ted Talk) 68–69
Mind Only 109
The Mindful Path to Self Compassion (Germer) 58–60
mindfulness *see* sati
Mindfulness (Goldstein) 160–161
moments of grace 72–73
morality 119–131
movement, rhythms of 68–69
murder 126–127
Nagarjuna (philosopher monk) 104–107
narcissistic wounds 88–89
'natural state' 164–165
nature of mind 114–115, 160–161, 168–169
   see also rigpa

nervous system 26–27, 30–31, 90, 110–111
nervous system and PTSD 26–27
Netherlands, Arnhem 70–71
neural networks *see* brain
nightmares 31–32
nirvana 94
Nixon, P. 48, 49
Noble Eightfold Path 127–128, 140
non-dual awakening 118
normality of emptiness 84
'not separate self-entities' 101–102
numbness 10, 71–72
objectless practice 162–163
objects of mindfulness 143–145
obsessive-compulsive wounds 89
oral wounds 88
overworking 44–45
   see also exhaustion
'Oxford' practice 165
paramita ('six perfections') 125–126
Parkes, C. M. 10
Pascal, B. 45
patience 125–126
Perfection of Wisdom 106–107
Perry, J. W. 64–65
philosophy/psychology 3–8
physical aspects of bereavement 21–37
physicality of emptiness 86
plasticity of brains 157–158
pleasure, absence of 91
post-traumatic stress disorder (PTSD) 26–27, 90, 110–111
Present Past 107–113
prisoners 74
protective mechanisms 30–31
protest 30–31
psychopathy 126–127
'pure vision' 112–113

Index

rage 30–31, 68–69
Rahula (Son of Buddha) 93–94
Rangdrol, S. T. 159
reality 102–103
 see also illusion
relax as it is 166–167
religion 3–4, 130–131
remorse 126–128
reorganization and recovery 10
resistant attachment 6
rhythms of movement 68–69
Ricard, M. 126–127
right concentration 140, 142–143
right effort 140–141
right mindfulness 141–142
rigpa (basic space of awareness) 159–169
Rinpoche, T. xxxi–xxxii
River of Change 100–107
Rogers, C. 65
Rosenberg, L. 56
Rosenmann, - 44
ruminating 134–135
Ryle, A. 7–8
Salzberg, S. 136
samadhi (concentration) 142–143
samana (spiritual dropout) 94
samsara 107
sangha (Three Jewels of Buddhism) 18, 19
sati (mindfulness) 5, 17–20, 27, 36–37, 129–131, 139–148
 emotions/truth 141–159
 generosity 125–126
 heart 55–56
 mind the gap process 65–66, 69–72, 74
 see also awareness
Satipatthana Sutta 27, 125–126

 see also sati
schizoid personality disorder 90
schizoid wounds 88
schizotypal personality disorder 90
'second arrow' 92
secure attachment 6
seeing clearly 111–113
self, emptiness 95–100
self-liberation 160–161
Sensorimotor Psychotherapy Institute 30
'separate self entity' 99–100
sexual abuse 29–30, 128
'shaky tenderness' 65–66
shamatha (calm abiding) 141–142
Shambhala Mountain Center retreat 65–66
shame 29–30, 91–92, 132–133
Shantideva (Buddhist monk) 130
shock 10, 15–16
Shunryu, S. R. 103–104, 117
shunyata *see* emptiness
sila (morality) 119–131
'six perfections' 125–126
skandhas/'five heaps'/aggregates 96, 177–178
somatic memories 111–112, 133–134
somatic movement therapy 52–53
spiritual emptiness 93–94
stages of life/grief 8–13
stealing 127–128
Still Water Mindfulness Practice Community 74
Stokes, T. 151
storehouse consciousness 109–111
stress 33–35, 44–45, 48–49
'suchness' 106–107
Suddodhana (Father of Buddha) 93–94

Index

suffering, duhkha of 82
sutras 102–103, 106–107, 113, 114–115
Suzuki, R. S. 132–134
symbiotic wounds 88–89
tathagatagarbha see buddha-nature
tathata 106–107
Ted Talks 68–69
Thich Nhat Hanh 18–19
   compassion 57
   courage 55
   loss and bereavement 27
   mind the gap process 68–69, 74
This Moment, This Only mantra 74–75
Thomas, C. 27
The Thought of the Heart (Hillman) 42
Three Jewels of Buddhism 18
'three natures' 111–112
'three root poisons' 128
'thusness' 106–107
trauma 25–27, 28–32, 88–89, 151–152, 158–159
Traumatic Stress (Van der Kolk) 28–29
Tree, I. 100–101
triggers of emotion 150–159
triggers of emptiness 85–86
truth 104–106, 149–159
Two Arrows 136–139
ultimate truth 104–106
unconditional friendliness (*maitri*) 17–18, 55–56, 73

unfabricated mindfulness 160–161
'unthought known' (Bollas) 66–67
Van der Kolk, B. 28–29
Vasubandhu (Buddhist monk) 109
vertical felt shift 155
vipashyana (insight) 141–142
walking mindfully 36–37
Way of the Bodhisattva (Shantideva) 130
Weller, F. 10–11, 15–16, 28, 40–41
Welwood, J. 155
What Freud Didn't Know (Stokes) 151
whole being and grief 13–17
The Wild Edge of Sorrow (Weller) 10–11, 15–16, 28, 40–41
Wilding (Tree) 100–101
Winnicott, D. W. 6
wisdom 125–126
Wohlleben, P. 100–101
The Words to Say It (Cardinale) 65
'worker heart' 39–60
wounds 88–89, 151–152, 158–159
Yasodhara (Wife of Buddha) 93–94
yearning and searching 10
Yoga Practice School 109, 111–112
Yogachara *see* Yoga Practice School
Young, S. 160–161
Zen 27, 115, 132–134

Further praise for *Present with Suffering*

"At a time when we face so much personal, collective and planetary loss and suffering, this book comes as a timely and welcome support, a reminder of how by staying present with our grief and pain we might find ways through to healing. Sharing from her own experience of deep loss, Elizabeth Wilde McCormick guides us gently through psychological, cultural and spiritual paths that can sustain us in the darkest times; she shows how the practice of mindfulness and, in particular, the Buddhist teachings of Thich Nhat Hanh open the heart. Nigel Wellings then lucidly outlines core Buddhist teachings to describe the development of wisdom, embracing and transforming feelings of emotional emptiness into an Buddhism describes the 'two wings' that enable the flight of awakening as 'wisdom and compassion'. This book truly is a gift for our troubled times."
Linda Hartley, author of *Somatic Psychology: Body, Mind and Meaning*

"This important book offers a heartfelt exploration into human suffering. By drawing on their personal experience of living and working with suffering, the authors offer a critical orientation of wisdom and hope for those navigating through the painful turbulences of loss, grief and trauma."
Margaret Landale MSc, psychotherapist, supervisor and speaker

"The question the authors pose is: How can we be with the things that hurt? Their answer is: through awareness, acceptance, kindness and compassion – the components of wisdom. By exploring bereavement through embodiment and narrative (McCormick), and offering an explanation of emptiness that is unusually faithful to both Buddhist and therapeutic understandings (Wellings), together they have produced a short book resonant with awareness, kindness, compassion and wisdom."
Gay Watson, Ph.D., author of *A Philosophy of Emptiness and Attention Beyond Mindfulness*

Further praise for *Present with Suffering*

"A thought-provoking meditation for everyone of being in the world, living in impermanence, emptiness and wholeness, and in harmony, with the help of Buddhist teachings. An invite for each of us to look at the essentials of what it means to be human. *Present with Suffering* teaches us to sit back in 'our observing awareness,' suggests how to 'fill the gap of emptiness,' and most of all, asks us to keep in mind the 'not necessarily so.'"
Marie-Anne Bernardy-Arbuz, clinical psychologist and CAT psychotherapist, Paris, France

"An absorbing exploration reconciling the human experience of suffering with the spiritual insights of meditative practice. Seen through the lenses of Buddhism and psychotherapy, the authors explain that within the bleakness of loss arises the possibility that pain and grief can be transformed into something new, more bearable and ultimately liberating."
Dr Sarah Eagger MB, BS, FRCPsych, Chair of the Janki foundation for Spirituality in Healthcare and former Consultant Psychiatrist at Imperial College London

"Wellings and Wilde McCormick provide contrasting yet complementary voices on this important topic. The seeming natural impulse can be to turn away from suffering, that it's all too much. Within these pages we are invited to not just turn towards and be with suffering in all its guises, but also to lean on ancient Buddhist practices in so doing. These practices allow for an intimate communion with the body-felt sense of pain beyond story, and ultimately, the dissolution of this pain in the basic goodness at the core."
Dr Andy Harkin, medical doctor and psychotherapist